Boosting Math Scores

Boosting Math Scores

by The Editors of
The World Book Encyclopedia

Published by

World Book Encyclopedia, Inc.
a Scott Fetzer company

Chicago

Special Consultant
Peter Pereira, M.A.
Assistant Professor
School of Education
DePaul University

Contents

Note to students

Most students want to do as well as they possibly can in school. One of the most important subjects—both in school and throughout life—is math.

The intent of *Boosting Math Scores* is to show you that math is not as mysterious or complicated as it may look. Perhaps with a better understanding of the subject, you will find yourself not only doing well, but enjoying math, too.

The book is divided into two parts. Part I, "Making math work," identifies common problems that people have with math. It offers specific suggestions for studying math, getting help when you need it, and preparing for and taking tests. Part I also gives tips for using a calculator, doing word problems, reading math, and using tables and graphs. Throughout Part I, you will find many pointers to help you organize your math thinking.

Part II, "Math basics," is meant to show you how much you already know about math and to help you identify areas where your understanding is weak. Self-tests and practice problems are included to help you measure your skills. There is also a glossary of math terms and a table of math symbols that you can use for quick reference. An annotated bibliography suggests other books you can go to for further information about improving your math skills.

There is one word of caution, however. The suggestions in this book are very useful. By learning new and more effective ways of approaching math, you can significantly improve your skills and understanding of math. But you cannot expect to see a dramatic improvement overnight, just from reading this book. You need to begin to *use* these suggestions in your everyday math study. If you do, you should begin to see a slow but steady improvement in your test scores. You may also see your interest in math grow as you become a more comfortable and confident math student.

Note to parents

Boosting Math Scores is a book for the whole family. While it is geared toward students, it can also be used by adults who would like tips for using math in everyday living. The book may also be used by students and their parents, working *together,* to help resolve difficulties in math.

Parents can help their children to use this book in a number of ways. First, by reading the book and knowing what's in it, parents can re-inforce many of the book's suggestions. In-cluded are many practical, effective methods for studying and thinking about math, along with tips for avoiding bad math habits. Parents can help their children break poor study habits and encourage more positive ways of learning math.

Another way parents can help is by trying to be available when their children need assist-ance with their homework. This does not mean hovering over them whenever they open their math books. It simply means creating an atmo-sphere in which children feel comfortable ask-ing for help if they need it. Of course, there are times when parents themselves may not be able to help. At such times, parents can encourage their children to seek out one of the other sources of help discussed in this book.

Parents can also help children, quite simply, by encouraging them to read this book. It is written at a level students can understand, and it is filled with ideas about math that many people never have considered before. Introducing students to these ideas may open some doors for them. It may help them to see math in new ways and gain confidence as math students.

This book also provides some reference material that may be helpful to both adults and students. For instance, if you forget how to find the area of a circle or how to find a percentage, the answers can be found in this book.

Both students and their parents can use this book to start some discussions about math. This may be a subject they've never talked about together before. Many parents feel uncertain about math themselves and feel unable to help their children. If you feel this way, read on. You will see that math is not an impossible subject. In fact, it can be a lot of fun.

Part I

Making math work

Identifying math trouble spots

Many people feel that math is a difficult subject for them. This is true of adults as well as students. It is interesting to note that many people who have trouble with math do quite well in other subject areas. So we are left with a puzzling question: Why does this area of study present problems for so many people?

One answer is that math is a very special subject. You cannot "read" math the way you read a story. And you cannot "look" at a math problem the way you would look at a picture.

If learning math is difficult for you, or if you would just like to do better in your math work but cannot seem to improve, you need to take a look at your math habits. You need to try to identify what is keeping you from doing as well in math as you would like.

Let's take a look at some common problems that cause trouble in studying math. As you read along, ask yourself if you have any of these problems. If you do, pay close attention to the suggestions for solving them.

Are you properly prepared for work?

Don't be too quick to say yes. Being properly prepared for math involves a lot more than it may for some other subjects.

First of all, whether you are reading your textbook, listening in class, or settling down to do your homework, you always need your math book, lots of clean paper, and at least two freshly sharpened pencils. Whenever you read about math or listen to an explanation, you need to take notes and try out problems. You need lots of paper because you do not know how much practicing and note taking will be necessary. If your work is too cramped together, you might not be able to read it later on. Be sure to have any other materials you need for the work you are doing, such as a ruler, a compass, or graph paper. A later section of this book, "Shaping up math study skills," offers further suggestions for preparing for math work.

Of course, you also must be mentally prepared to work. Part of your mental preparation is being sure you understand what was done in class the day before. This brings us to another important problem that many people have.

Do you understand that math builds on itself?

Each new math concept you learn depends on your understanding math concepts that you learned earlier. You cannot learn to subtract if you do not know how to add. You cannot learn to divide if you do not know how to multiply. In order to understand what is being done in your math class today, you must understand what was done yesterday. Each time you learn something new, it connects to what you have learned before.

Many students overlook the fact that math builds on itself. When they come to something difficult, they think, "This is boring (or too hard). I'll skip it and go on to the next thing. I'll never need to know this anyhow." These students are making a serious mistake. Whatever you are learning in math, remember that you *will* need to know it again, quite likely the very next day. You must master each skill before you attempt to go on to the next one. Learning math is like climbing the steps on a ladder. If you try to skip a step and leap up to the next one, you just might slip and fall.

Are you missing a piece of the puzzle?

For many students, math is difficult because they have skipped a step on the ladder. For one reason or another, they have missed learning some basic math concepts. If you think this is your problem, you need to try to identify the missing pieces that are keeping you from putting together the math puzzle.

If you are aware of specific areas of math that you have always had trouble with, then go back and learn them as soon as possible. It may mean extra work now, but you will save yourself a lot of extra work in the future.

If you are not quite sure where your math strengths and weaknesses lie, try taking the self-tests in Part II, "Math basics." The self-tests may help you identify the types of problems you need to work on. Once you know what pieces are missing, you can go back and try to fill them in.

Do you think there is only one right way to solve each problem?

When it comes to math, many people think that there is only one correct way to do any particular problem. In many cases, this just isn't true. A great many types of math problems can be solved by several different methods.

For example, it is possible to add a column of figures in several ways. You might add from the top down, or you might add from the bottom up. You also might add, in any order you wish, groups of numbers that seem to go together. For instance, you might group numbers that add up to 10 (6 + 4 or 3 + 7). Or you might first add all the 5's before adding the other numbers. It does not matter how you add the numbers together, as long as you find the correct total. Look at this example:

$$
\begin{array}{r}
6 \\
8 \\
+4 \\
\hline
\end{array}
$$

You could add these figures in three different ways:

$6 + 8 = 14 + 4 = 18$
$4 + 8 = 12 + 6 = 18$
$6 + 4 = 10 + 8 = 18$

Other types of math problems, particularly word problems, can also be done in any way that works for you. You may have already noticed that different teachers explain ideas in different ways. And sometimes your teacher explains an idea differently than the book does. This should tell you that there is often more than one correct way to work a problem.

Many students are afraid they are doing something wrong if they do a problem differently than they were shown. Actually, it's fine to do problems your own way—as long as it leads to the correct answer. In fact, many times students find ways to do problems that are easier for them than the ways they were shown. The section on "Developing good math habits" talks more about using short cuts, patterns, and estimates to find easier ways to work problems.

Do you ask for help soon enough?

If you don't understand something you have been shown in math, try to get help right away. If you do not completely understand each math concept before going on to the next, math will only get harder and harder for you.

Students who do not learn some math concepts—and then try to go on without understanding—can end up feeling lost and upset when they try to do their math work. The only way they can solve this problem is to go all the way back to learn the concepts they missed. The longer they wait to get help, the harder it is to catch up.

As soon as you come to something that doesn't make sense to you, ask for help. Don't wait! The difficulty will only get worse, not better. A later section on "Getting help" will tell you more about how, when, and where to get help with math.

Do you understand how to read the language of math?

Many students think that they can sit down and read a math book the same way they would read any other book. But reading math requires special skills. Math books contain many special words whose meanings you must learn. You must also read much more carefully and slowly than you would most other books. And you must have paper and pencil ready to try working out problems.

The section on "Reading the language of math" offers some specific suggestions. If you have problems understanding math language, be sure to read that section carefully.

Are you afraid or anxious about math?

Some people say they simply don't like math. Others say that they feel nervous or uneasy or even afraid when they have to do math. Some people feel so anxious that just looking at numbers makes their minds go blank. Or when a teacher starts talking about how to do a problem, they start to daydream and miss the whole explanation. Do you know any students like this?

Suppose, for example, that Jill was absent on the day her class learned how to divide one fraction by another fraction. If Jill does not get someone to explain this procedure to her, she may feel lost every time it comes up. Most students learn to divide fractions in fifth or sixth grade. If Jill doesn't learn the concept then, from that point on there will be a big hole in her understanding of mathematics. Whenever she has to do problems that are connected in any way with division of fractions, she may feel confused and lost. And if the same thing should happen with several other math concepts, before long Jill may start to think of mathematics as a confusing subject. She may begin to be afraid to tackle it and soon may see herself as a person who "can't do math." The most obvious way to avoid this fear of math is to never go on to a new step until you understand the step before it.

Some people are afraid of math just because they once had a problem with it. Now, even though they have gotten over their past troubles, they still think of themselves as people who can't do math. If this is your problem, you might find that taking the self-tests in Part II, "Math basics," will help you see that you know more about math than you think you do. That should make it easier to begin thinking of yourself as a person who *can* do math. If you find instead that there *are* some gaps in your math education, you will then know where to fill in so that you don't have to feel so uneasy about math in the future.

Still another reason why some people are afraid of math is that they set up unrealistic standards for themselves. They think they should be able to find answers more quickly; that they should never make mistakes; that they shouldn't have to reread an explanation. These ideas produce needless fears in people. Even professional mathematicians sometimes count on their fingers or draw pictures to help themselves understand problems. They do reread explanations—and even make mistakes.

Just learn to give yourself a chance to figure things out. Try to learn every step along the way—and be patient with yourself. If you start with trying to identify your math trouble spots, you have taken the first step toward overcoming them and becoming a better math student.

Developing good math habits

We've already talked about some ways of approaching the study of math that can cause problems for math students. Now we would like to suggest some *good* math habits—those that are crucial to your success in math. If you develop these habits, you should begin to feel more comfortable with math and do better in this subject.

1. Do neat and orderly work.

We all know that neatness counts. But in math, neatness counts for a lot more than you might think. The purpose of neatness in math is a lot more than having papers that look nice. In math, doing neat and orderly work can help you think more clearly and avoid careless errors.

First, neat work is easier to read—both for you and for your teacher. Allow plenty of space for each problem that you work. Then you can go back through a problem to check your work, to find your errors, or to remind yourself how to do a problem correctly.

Keep columns of numerals straight, whether you are adding, subtracting, multiplying, or dividing. Always be sure of the place value of the digits; you can only add ones to ones, tens to tens, and so on. If you let your columns wobble, you might make the mistake of adding a one in the tens column, for example.

Write out all the steps in a problem—especially when you are first learning and practicing a new type of problem. This helps you be sure that you have not forgotten a step—and that you have worked through the steps in the correct order. It also makes it easier for you to go back and check for errors.

A jumbled, disordered, and hard-to-read paper only adds a sense of confusion to your work. Doing neat and orderly work makes it easier for you to think clearly. It is a crucial habit to develop if you want to be a successful math student.

2. Try to understand basic concepts.

Many people have the idea, beginning with the early grades of school, that the main object in math is to get the right answers to problems. Of course it is important to get the right answers. But that should not be your only goal —or even your main goal. Getting the right answer to a problem is almost a secondary goal. It proves that you have accomplished the main goal, which is to understand the basic math concept.

You can get the answer to a subtraction problem only if you understand the concept of subtraction. To do this you must go back to addition. Addition is putting together two parts to get a whole. Subtraction is the inverse or reverse of addition. You have the whole and one part, and you have to find the missing part.

Understanding the concept of multiplication works the same way. You have to go back to addition. If you understand the concept of addition, you can understand that multiplication is a short way to add when all the numbers are alike.

These are some very simple concepts, but the idea that you must understand concepts applies to all areas of math. In fact, the further along you get in math, the more important it is to understand the concepts behind what you are doing. As the rules become more complex, it becomes much more difficult to just memorize the rules. They will have no meaning for you if you don't understand the concepts on which the rules are based. If you develop the habit of understanding the reasons behind what you are doing in math, the right answers will come next.

3. Ask questions when they first occur.

The only way to feel comfortable with math is to know what's going on. If you go to class and do not understand what the teacher is explaining that day, you must ask about it immediately or as soon as possible. Many seemingly complicated points in math can be cleared up fairly easily if you don't wait too long to ask.

Very often students don't ask questions because they are afraid other people in the class will think they are slow or will laugh at them. The truth is, though, that almost any time you have a question, other students in the class have the same question. They would probably be relieved to hear someone ask it. It is really best if you can ask in class so other students can benefit from your question. But if this is not possible, ask your teacher or a friend or *anyone* who would know, just as soon as you can. Some possible sources of help are discussed in another section of this book, "Getting help."

4. Memorize basic facts and rules.

Even though you must first understand the underlying concepts, there are some mathematical facts that must be memorized if you are to be successful in this subject. Having certain memorized facts at hand can save a tremendous amount of time—especially when you need to do problems within a time limit.

Memorizing facts is like developing reflexes. You can respond to some problems almost automatically, without stopping to think or working out the same simple problems over and over again.

Here are some of the basic mathematical facts that you should memorize:

basic addition facts
basic subtraction facts
multiplication tables
squares of common numbers
decimal equivalents of common fractions
basic measurement equivalents
formulas for perimeter, area, volume

Of course, you have already memorized a great many of these facts. You have been working on them over the years, going back to your addition facts in the first grade. But a surprising number of students have not completely accomplished the task. They may believe they know their multiplication tables, but they still occasionally get stuck on 8×7 or 7×9.

If you have trouble remembering some of the basic facts, you know what a handicap it can be. It cuts into your ability to finish tests on time and to get good grades on them. It also lengthens the time it takes to do your nightly homework assignments.

Fortunately, it is never too late. You can still go back and memorize the facts you need to know. Make flashcards for the facts you have trouble remembering. Then practice with them. Get a friend or a parent to test you. Learn those basic facts! You will find that knowing them not only helps you work faster, but also aids you in seeing patterns and short cuts and in estimating—other helpful time-saving techniques.

Along with memorizing basic facts, you should also memorize the right ways to solve certain problems. These are the "rules" you have been taught over and over again. Still, some people forget them. For example, do you remember how to find a least common denominator for two fractions? Or do you have to figure it out again each time you do it?

Some memorizing is unavoidable in math. Know what you have to memorize, and do it. It may take some time now, but you will be paid back in the time you save whenever you do math problems—for the rest of your life.

5. Look for patterns and short cuts.

Mathematics is not only computing and memorizing. In fact, many mathematicians dislike computation and will do anything possible to avoid it. They are far more interested in studying patterns wherever they can find them— patterns in words, patterns in shapes, patterns in shells, and especially patterns in arithmetic.

"This is all very well," you may say, "for the

mathematician. But I am just a student looking for help in arithmetic or algebra. What do patterns have to do with boosting my scores in math?" A great deal, as it turns out. It is hard to memorize something that makes no sense to you. It takes a long time, and once memorized, it is easy to forget. But if you see patterns in what you are doing and make connections to other things, then you will be able to remember them more easily. Better yet, you will be able to recall them, even if you haven't practiced them for a while.

Think about how you learned the multiplication table. You probably found that 5 times any number is pretty easy; the answer always ends in 0 or 5. Two times anything is also quite simple; even little children know how to count by 2's. But there are other patterns that might have helped you learn the multiplication table. Do you remember the 9's?

9, 18, 27, 36, 45, 54, 63, 72, 81

Did you ever notice that when you add the two digits in these multiples of 9, you always get 9? This makes the 9's much easier to memorize. The 7's also have a pattern that is interesting, but we will give you only a hint. Look at the last digit of the numbers in the multiples of 7:

7, 14, 21, 28, 35, 42, 49, 56, 63

When you read these backward, do you see any pattern that has to do with the answers you get when you multiply by 3?

3, 6, 9, 12, 15, 18, 21, 24, 27

Of course, you probably already know the multiplication table. But patterns crop up all over the place in arithmetic and algebra. If you spot these patterns, you can use them as short cuts to avoid a lot of tedious calculation. And most people enjoy math more when they use patterns and short cuts. Your answers may also be more accurate, and you may remember facts longer.

Let's look at a couple of examples. Can you find a short cut to help you add these numbers?

$$13 + 26 + 37 + 24 =$$

Remember that you can add these numbers in any order you like. What if you added them like this?

$$13 + 37 = 50$$
$$26 + 24 = 50$$

If you notice these two pairs of numbers that add up to 50, the problem becomes simply $50 + 50 = 100$. Then you can do the addition in your head, rather than writing out the problem and adding each column separately.

Can you find a short cut in this problem?

$$3 \cdot 15 + 7 \cdot 15 =$$

This problem asks you to add 3 fifteens and 7 fifteens. You can add 3 and 7 in your head and find that the answer is 10 fifteens, or 150. It would take much longer to multiply 3 times 15 and 7 times 15 and then add the two products together.

As you look through your textbook or do your homework, see if you can find problems that can be done quickly by spotting short cuts. Not all problems are like this, but many of them are. Try your hand at some of the problems that follow. (There are more examples in the unit on "Using a calculator.") None of these problems requires brute-force calculation. If you cannot find a short cut or two in each one, get someone to help you find them. (The answers to these problems are in the answer key at the back of the book.)

1. $64 - 50 + 6 =$
2. 75% of 12 =
3. $5 \cdot 4 \cdot 3 \cdot 2 \cdot 1 =$
4. $8.2 - 9 + 4 - 1.2 =$
5. $\frac{1}{3} \cdot 11 + \frac{1}{3} \cdot 4 =$
6. $\frac{(51.3)^2}{51.3} =$
7. $(84.2 - 2.3)(36 \cdot 5 - 18 \cdot 10) =$
8. $\frac{(77)(12)}{33} =$

Whenever you see a pattern, it is worth looking into it. Try to figure out why it occurs, how it can help you remember something, or how it connects with something else you know. There is bound to be some significance. Find it, and you will have done something to help yourself understand math better.

6. Use estimating as a tool.

If you have memorized the basic facts and rules, it will be easier to see patterns and short cuts that will allow you to estimate in your math work. But what do we mean by *estimating*?

Actually, estimating is something you do all the time in the course of your everday living. Estimating is really nothing more than reasonable guessing. Suppose, for example, that you have a baby-sitting job that is going to last $5\frac{1}{2}$ hours and that you will be paid \$2.20 an hour. You wonder how much you will earn. Obviously \$120 would be a ridiculous guess and so would \$1.20. But you know that 2×5 is 10. And you know that you will be sitting for a little more than 5 hours and earning a little more than \$2 an hour. So a guess of about \$12 would be more reasonable. If you actually calculate the exact answer, you will see that the estimate was pretty close.

Estimate = about \$12.00
$5\frac{1}{2} \times \$2.20 = \$12.10$

There are other times when you estimate because there simply is no point in getting the exact answer. Suppose you want to triple a recipe that calls for $1\frac{1}{2}$ pounds of flour. How many pounds of flour should you buy? You may as well estimate 5 pounds, since 5 pounds is a common packaging weight for flour, and you probably won't need more than that amount. Watch yourself over the next few days to see how many times you actually guess at things rather than calculating exact answers. Are your guesses usually reasonable?

You may be wondering what all this has to do with math study. Actually, estimating—making *reasonable* guesses (not wild guesses)—is a very important part of learning math. Many people do not realize this. They think they must always get an exact answer. Or they think the teacher will be angry if they guess. Or they may think people estimate answers only when they don't know how to work the problems. All of these ideas are incorrect. Estimating has many valid uses.

Estimating is an essential step in working some types of problems. Long division is a good example. Suppose you need to divide 2,836 by 13. It is helpful to guess that the answer probably starts with 2 (since 28 divided by 13 is about 2). If you had to do this problem, you would probably begin by trying a 2 without even realizing that you are estimating.

Estimating an answer can also help you avoid mistakes. For example, if you had to multiply 9.8 by 10.1, an answer that wasn't close to 100 wouldn't make much sense. You estimate here by using a mental short cut. Of course, you need to know that 10×10 is 100 and that 9.8 is almost 10, or you will not be able to make a reasonable guess. So it is absolutely necessary that you have memorized your basic facts and understand your basic concepts if you want to make helpful and accurate guesses.

You can also use estimating to help you when you get stuck. If you don't know how to get an exact answer, you can make a guess. Then you can check to see if your guess seems reasonable. Once you have an idea of what a reasonable answer might be, you sometimes can see how to get an exact answer. This is especially useful for figuring out word problems.

Estimating is a valuable tool for doing math. It can help you to get to the right answers. It can save you time in your work. You probably use it often without even realizing that you are doing so. Now that you have thought more about it, try using estimating even more often in your daily assignments.

Shaping up math study skills

Developing and using good study skills is important in every subject, but it is crucial in math. Using good math study skills can help you make the most of your time both when working in the classroom and when studying at home.

Your attitude when you are studying math is every bit as important as your study skills. Your goal should be to understand as much as you can about math concepts. You should not just try to get through the class period or finish your homework assignment. You should concentrate on trying to learn the concepts and trying to become comfortable working the problems. Your success in math can improve tremendously if you keep this goal in mind.

Working in the classroom

Here are some guidelines you can follow that will help you make the most out of your time in math class.

Be prepared. It is essential that you come prepared for the work you are doing in math class. First of all, you need to bring paper, pencils, and your math books with you. Bring any other tools you will need for the day's work—a compass, a ruler, a protractor, or graph paper. If you don't have all your supplies, you will be unable to take notes, work problems, and follow what the teacher is saying.

Second, being prepared means having your homework done before class begins. Since math builds on itself, you must understand what was done yesterday in order to learn today's lesson. Doing your homework is one way of being sure that you really understand each step before going on to the next one.

When you get to class it is important that you find a seat where you can see the board and hear the teacher. If the teacher assigns the seats and the one you get is not good for you, politely ask for a change.

Be a good listener. Listening is a skill. You aren't necessarily listening just because you're in class and your eyes and ears are open. In order to truly listen, you must actively participate in what is going on.

First, look at the teacher as you listen. Always try to make sense out of what you are hearing. In math class, this means connecting what you are hearing now with what you have learned before. Ask yourself: "What directions are being given?" "What procedures am I to follow?" "Do I understand all the words and symbols?" If you do not know the answers to these questions, ask as soon as possible.

Second, learn to filter out distractions. Don't listen to the workers outside your window or to the student tapping a pencil on the other side of the room. There will always be something going on besides the lesson. You can even be distracted by your own thoughts popping into your mind that keep your from concentrating on your math. Whenever any of these distractions get in the way, you must shut them off quickly and get your mind back to what your teacher or other students are saying. If you miss even a few words while you are daydreaming or listening to something else, you may get confused and need outside help to get back on the track.

Third, take notes! You may not be able to write down everything the teacher says, but get as much as you can of the most important instructions. If it is possible, write down everything the teacher puts on the board. When a teacher writes a term or a solution to a problem on the board, this is usually a clue that the word or the solution is important for you to learn. Also, jot down any questions you have that you are not able to ask at once. Then try to get those questions answered some time before you leave school and attempt to do your homework.

Taking notes is important because you can't remember everything, especially instructions which you may need later. Also, it is likely that you will be studying other subjects in other classes before you get back to doing your math homework. If you have no notes, you may forget some important points about how to do the work.

Finally, be sure to listen carefully to other students in your class as well as to your teacher. Often another student will ask a question that you've been wanting to ask yourself. Other times, another student may come up with a new idea or explain something in a way that will help you understand a math concept better.

Doing homework

If you wish to succeed in your math studies, it is absolutely necessary that you do your math homework faithfully. Doing your homework is one way to check if you understand the concept that was taught that day. If you have problems with your homework, you know that you need to ask for help. On the other hand, if your homework goes smoothly and you are able to do all the problems, then you can feel fairly certain that you have learned the day's lesson.

Find a quiet place for study. In order to do your homework, you need a place to work where you can concentrate. That means there should be as few distractions as possible. Some people say they work better with music or the television on. You may be able to do math under these conditions and get by all right. But the truth is that most people work much better when there are few distractions. If you can work in front of the television, you can work even better and faster with the television off. You must concentrate on only one thing: your math homework. So find a *quiet* place to work.

Your place for studying should also have a desk or table that is large enough for you to spread out your books and materials. You need a good light that is bright but not glaring. The light should shine on your work, not in your eyes. And you need to work in a comfortable temperature. You're better off if it's a little cool. If you're too warm, you may feel sleepy and want to stop working.

Be properly prepared. Having a good place to work is a beginning, but having the right materials and a good attitude is also important. You should always write down your math assignment when it is given in class. Then be sure to bring the written assignment home, along with your books and notes. Even if the homework problems are not in your book, you may need to look at your book for a reminder of how to do them. Remember, it is far better to have your math book with you, even if you don't need it, than it is to find you need an explanation that's in a textbook or notebook that you left in your locker at school.

Besides your books and notes, you should have all your other homework equipment with you when you sit down to work. That means paper, pencils with erasers and sharp points, rulers, and any other tools you might be using at the time. Have enough paper so that you can give each problem as much room as it needs. Work neatly and show all your steps so it will be easier to go back and check your answers. Have scrap paper handy for checking your answers and for trying out any ideas you might have for working the problems in other ways.

Try to approach your work with an attitude that you will learn as much as you can. Decide on the time that you will begin your math homework, and when that time comes, do it. Don't put homework off because you are uninspired or in a bad mood. If you seriously begin to form the habit of doing your math at a certain time every day, you will soon be able to sit down and do it without delay. But also remember to give yourself breaks. Work for no more than 25 to 45 minutes, and then rest for a while. If you were really concentrating for that long, you will have earned a break. After 5 or 6 minutes of walking around, stretching a bit, or eating a small snack, you will feel refreshed and able to study again. You will be much more likely to enjoy doing the work and to get it done correctly.

Follow a study plan.   It helps to know the right way to get started on your homework. Begin by reading the section in your book that goes with the exercises. Then reread the notes you took in class that day, including any sample problems your teacher wrote on the board. Then look at the sample problems given at the beginning of the exercise. Make sure you understand how to do the samples before starting the exercise.

After all this, you will be ready to start doing the problems in your assignment. Some books give the answers to odd-numbered or even-numbered problems. Do those problems first and check your answers. Then you will know if you are on the right track. If questions come up while you are working, jot them down so you will remember to ask the teacher to answer them the next day.

If, despite this organized approach, you are still unable to complete your homework, you might need to ask for help in learning the math concept you are working on. Another section of this book discusses how to know when you need help—and where to get it.

Reading the language of math

In many ways, mathematics has a language all its own. Certainly math textbooks are not like most other kinds of books, whether they be textbooks in other subjects or books you read for pleasure. Knowing how to read a math book can be a big help in boosting your math scores.

How to read a math book

When you sit down to read your math textbook, you are doing something that is quite different from reading a novel, the newspaper, or even a history text. Math books must be approached in a special way. If you know *how* to read math books, they will not seem so difficult—and you will find it much easier to deal with them.

Familiarize yourself with your math book. Before you even start using a new math book, look it over carefully. See how the material is presented in each chapter. As you look over the book, find the answers to the following questions:

Where are the sample problems and their answers?
Are there answers in the back for even-numbered or odd-numbered exercise problems?
Are there practice tests?

Is there a glossary of terms?
Is there a table of math symbols?
Does the book have an index?
Is there a bibliography of books you can turn to for extra help?

You might practice this familiarizing skill by answering these questions for the book you are reading right now. Knowing what is in the book—and where everything is—can save you time later on.

Read slowly and carefully. Adjust to a slow reading pace whenever you are studying math. Also, accept the fact that you may have to reread a paragraph or a sample problem several times before you fully understand it. Do not let the fact that you must read slowly and reread make you think that you are not a good math student. Even experts in mathematics need to reread and slow down when they read about math ideas.

Be an active reader. In order to understand what you are reading in a math textbook, you have to participate in what you are reading. You cannot just pass your eyes over the words as you might with a light novel or a book of jokes. You must constantly question the material.

Reading actively also means that you must always have paper and pencil with you when you read a math book. You can't just read the explanations without trying the problems. There is no way to learn math without practicing it. If you try to just read it, you will not really remember what you have read.

Take notes.   Taking notes helps you organize and remember what you are reading. If you are learning how to change decimals to per cent, for instance, jot down the steps that you have to remember In order to work the problems. Writing down the important ideas will help you remember them.

Try some practice problems.   If you can do these, you can feel pretty confident that you understand the work. The answers should be provided for all the sample problems and are often given for either the even-numbered or odd-numbered exercise problems. Try a few problems for which answers are provided. If you are not getting the right answers, you need to go back and read the explanation again or ask someone for help.

Keep your concentration up.   When you are reading a math book, you have to concentrate. So pick your study time and place carefully. Choose a time when you are alert, not sleepy. And find a place where you will not be disturbed and where the lighting is good.

Make math connections.   Every time you are reading about a new math concept, try to connect it to the last concept you learned. This will help you keep in mind the total picture of what you are learning. In math, you must always be able to draw the connections from one skill to the next.

The special vocabulary of math

If reading math books is difficult for you, it might be because of the words that are in them. It's not that the vocabulary is so difficult to read or pronounce. But math sometimes uses words in very special ways.

One problem is that often math uses words that you already know, but in a different way. For example, the words *positive* and *negative*, when referring to numbers, do not mean the same thing that they do in everyday conversations. In math, these words have different meanings than you use if you say that you are *positive* that you are right about something, or that you have *negative* feelings about someone.

Another problem is that math words are often used with more precise meanings than we are used to. For example, *non-negative* is not the same as *positive*, since zero is a non-negative number. And *zero* is not the same as *nothing;* zero is a very special number with special properties. A *triangle* consists of three line segments; it does not include the points (or the area) inside the triangle. In ordinary (non-math) language, we might think of a triangle as a shape that includes the area inside its borders. In math, the word *triangle* is given a much more exact definition.

When you recognize a word in a math book, and it doesn't seem to mean what you've always thought it meant, read the explanation carefully. Check the glossary or a dictionary, or ask someone to explain the meaning to you. You should give the same treatment to words that are brand new to you.

If you remember that math uses language in a different way, and if you keep your mind open to learning new meanings of words, you will find it easier to use the language of math. (A glossary at the back of this book provides the meanings of some of the most commonly used math terms.)

Reading and following instructions

Being able to read and follow instructions is a skill that goes hand in hand with success in math. Most of the material in your math book *is* instructions on how to do something. The general rules for reading math apply here: read everything carefully; think and question while you're reading; look up any words you don't understand; and practice doing the problems as you go along.

Always make sure that you read and understand the instructions before you start to work. This usually means that you will need to read them more than once. It is not unusual to have to read directions two or three times before you start to work. Don't be in a hurry! It will take less time in the long run if you make sure you understand what you are expected to do, than if you rush ahead, make mistakes, and have to do the work over.

Taking math tests

Tests! We all have to take them, and in every subject, too. But many students get especially nervous about taking math tests. There is something about looking at that sheet full of problems, and knowing that there is a limited time in which to do them, that can make some math students' knees shake.

But this does not have to be so. The way to keep from getting that nervous feeling when you look at a math test is to go into the test properly prepared.

Preparing for math tests

Your preparation for math tests starts as soon as you start to take a math course. At the beginning of the school year, you should prepare a study plan for every subject, which will estimate how much time you will spend each day on all your homework. The amounts will probably be different for each subject. Some subjects are more demanding than others, and some are more difficult for you than others. Math may likely be a subject that needs more time, especially if it is a problem subject for you.

Once you have made your study plan, do your best to stick to it. If you study your math for a set period of time each day, you will not be forced to cram when it comes to test time. *Cramming* is waiting until the last day and then trying to memorize in a few hours what you should have learned over a period of weeks or months.

Cramming may force you to go into the test overtired and confused. Even if you are able to remember enough information to help on the test, cramming does not help your learning in the long run. Generally, people very quickly forget information they have crammed. And in math, you need to remember the concepts you studied for one test if you want to do well on the next one. The best way to prepare for a math test is to learn the math concepts by studying consistently, over a long period of time.

Say you have allowed yourself 30 to 45 minutes every day for math. Naturally you will spend a good portion of this time on your homework assignment for that day. But always use some time for reviewing concepts that you have learned earlier.

If you review on a regular basis, you should not need much extra study before a test. Since math builds on itself, you cannot allow yourself to get behind. So math tests should be the easiest to study for, since the nature of the subject practically forces you to be prepared at all times.

Studying for a math test with a friend or with a group of friends can be a good idea. A few students studying together can often help each other remember the concepts they have learned. You can test each other on these concepts and check each other's work. But it is important that you choose friends who are serious about studying. If the study session turns into a party, you would have been much better off studying alone.

Although your major preparation takes place over a long period of time, there are some special things that you should remember to do right before a test. First, it is helpful to go over all the concepts the night before the test. This does not mean cramming; you've already learned what you need for the test. But you should take about a half-hour to review and work a few simple problems. Make sure that you know how to do every type of problem that might appear on the test.

The next thing you should do is get a good night's sleep. This is very important! Avoid scheduling any big social activities, which might keep you out late, on the night before a test. If you are tired when you go in to take the test, you will be unable to think clearly or to work the math problems as quickly as you need to.

Another important matter is nutrition. Start your test day with a good breakfast. But do not overeat right before taking a test. If you have too much food in your stomach, your body will need lots of energy for digestion and may leave you with less energy for thinking. This will make you sluggish, and you will feel more like taking a nap than taking a test.

So what should you eat? Most studies have shown that a light meal containing some protein is best. But don't attempt to take a test on an empty stomach. You need the energy that food gives you, not only for thinking, but also for having the stamina to stay alert during the test.

Taking math tests

Even if you've done everything you could to get ready, you still may feel nervous when test time comes. It is not unusual to feel a little nervous when the tests are being handed out. But you will feel less nervous if you can say, "I'm prepared for this test. I've done everything I could to get ready, so I have nothing to worry about."

Here are some useful tips to keep in mind when taking a math test:

1. *Be on time.* If you are late for the test, you will lose valuable time. Even if you are right on time but have had to rush to make it, you will be out of breath, exhausted, even confused when the test starts. This may put you at a disadvantage. You may need some time to calm down while your mind rushes over the events that caused your lateness. Getting yourself together could rob you of several minutes of test-taking time. It is far better to be a few minutes early. Then you will have time to relax your mind and body before the test begins.

2. *Bring all the necessary supplies.* Find out beforehand what you will need. Bring several sharpened pencils with erasers. Ask your teacher ahead of time whether you will answer the problems on your own paper. Even if the answers are to be written on the test itself, you may still need work space. Ask whether you will be allowed to use scratch paper or if your teacher prefers that you do your scratch work on the test itself. If you will need scratch paper, make sure to bring it.

3. *Follow all directions exactly as they are given.* Misunderstanding directions is a common cause of errors on math tests. Be sure to listen to any oral instructions given by the teacher. Then read the general instructions at the top of the test at least twice. Be sure you understand the directions for each test item. If you have any questions, raise your hand and ask for help.

4. *Skim over the test.* You need to get an idea of how to budget your time. Check to see if some problems are worth more points than others. If so, allow more time for doing the problems that are worth more points. As soon as you have an overview of the test, begin working the problems. Be sure to read any special directions given for different sections of the test.

5. *Work all the problems that you know first.* Skip any problems that you don't understand. After you have done all the problems that you can answer easily, go back and try to work out the others. This way you will be sure to get credit for the answers you know.

6. *Check your answers at least once.* If possible, budget time at the end of the test to check your answers again. Anyone can make a careless mistake. For every error you can find and correct, you have saved yourself some points.

7. *Work at your own pace.* Don't try to keep up with anyone else. In fact, don't even look at anyone else. Keep all of your attention on your

own test paper. Don't waste any of your energy worrying about what others are doing.

8. Use your scored test as a study guide.

Here is a final but important point to remember about taking math tests. Tests are given for two reasons. They are given to help the teacher check your progress. But they are also intended to help *you* learn. When your graded test is returned to you, go over all the answers. Look to see what errors you made. Be sure you understand how to correct those errors. If your teacher does not go over the answers with the class, take it upon yourself to find out what caused your errors. Then use this opportunity to learn from your mistakes. Go back and work on any math concepts you didn't understand well. Remember that you will need to know them again and again as you go on in your study of math.

You might check your paper with those of your friends. They may understand how to work some problems you missed. Or make an appointment with your teacher so he or she can explain how to do any problems you don't understand. But whatever you do, don't go on to the next chapter unless you thoroughly understand this work. Use math tests to help yourself check your learning before you attempt to go on.

Getting help

Almost every math student needs help at some time. Sooner or later all students come to questions they cannot answer, problems they cannot work, or concepts they fail to understand at once. What should math students do when this happens? They should get help.

When to get help

It is important to realize when you need help. When you do not understand a math concept, even if it seems like a minor point, you need to ask for help *at once!* Remember that math concepts connect to each other. If, at any point, you fail to understand a concept, you may run into trouble whenever that concept, or anything connected to it, comes up.

You have learned that it is important to make sure you understand each day's work as you go along. If you wait until just before an exam and then try to catch up, you will have too much to learn in too short a time. You may have to go back to the point where you first had trouble and start over from there. Obviously, the sooner you get help, the less material you will have to repeat in order to get back up to where you belong.

Where to get help

There are many people who are willing and

able to help you when you have trouble with math. But you have to know who they are and how to approach them. Some students do not get help soon enough because they are afraid to ask or do not know who to ask. Here are some sources of help that are available to most students.

Friends and classmates. You may be surprised to see friends and classmates mentioned as your first source of help. Actually, they are often a good source. They are the easiest to find and work with. You may think that asking a friend or classmate for help with math would be a waste of time. Or you may think that doing your homework with a friend would be cheating. This is not true—if you work together in the right way.

If one study mate is just supplying answers to the other, then working together is a bad idea. But if both of you are doing your own work and trying to learn math concepts, you can gain a lot by working together.

A good way to start is for each of you to work through the assignment alone, doing all of the problems or as many as you understand how to do. Then you are ready to talk about the assignment. Your study mate may have taken different notes in class than you did and may be able to answer some of your questions. You may be able to explain how to solve a problem your partner is stuck on. Or you may find that both of you are confused about the same idea or problem. In that case it may be reassuring to know that your study mate and perhaps others are having the same difficulty. Also, you may realize that the point is probably a crucial one, if both of you have questions about it. Working together, you may be able to figure it out or to decide on the right questions to ask the teacher.

Above all, choose a study mate who is as concerned as you are about learning the math concepts—not just about getting the answers. If each of you is trying to learn and trying to share what you know, you should both improve your understanding of math.

Teachers. Of course, teachers should be an early line of help for you. Your teachers can help you the most if you let them know when you have a question or a problem. You can prevent small questions from turning into large problems simply by raising your hand immediately and asking a question whenever the teacher says something you don't understand. If this is impossible, then try to see the math teacher after class. The sooner you get any confusion cleared up, the better.

Sometimes you may need to spend more than just a few minutes with the teacher. In this case, it is best to make an appointment to see the teacher before or after school, during a break, or at recess. Teachers want to help you, but they have many students to think about and many other responsibilities—planning lessons, grading papers, and keeping records. You know before anyone else does when you have questions or need help. You must take the responsibility of asking your teacher for help. Do not wait for the teacher to tell you that you need it.

When you go to an appointment with your teacher, be prompt! The teacher may have a limited amount of time to spend with you, and you don't want to waste any of it. Bring your math books, notes, paper, and pencils with you. Be prepared to tell your teacher exactly what you don't understand. Have your assignment with you so your teacher can go over your work, step by step, and help you find where the trouble lies.

Your teacher can be a great help to you when approached in the right way. Make an appointment as soon as you begin to have difficulties. Then go to your conference prepared to work, with definite questions in mind.

Family members. Sometimes you may think you understand your math homework. Then when you get home and get started on it, you may find that you do not understand it as well as you thought you did. That's when you might try asking someone in your family for help. If you have a parent, brother, or sister who feels comfortable with math, he or she may be able to help you out in a pinch.

Of course, your family members also have lots of other things to do, so it's a good idea to give them some warning. You might say, "Mom, I'm having some trouble with my math assignment. Could you help me when you're finished with what you're doing?" Or, "Will you have a chance some time tonight to help me with my math homework, Sis?" Naturally it's best if you have not left your homework for the last minute. Then you can wait until someone is free to give you full attention. If you often need help with your homework, it would be wise to look at your assignment early to see if you might need help. Then arrange a time when someone can help you, and work on your other subjects in the meantime.

A word of caution: Remember and understand that your family may not always be able to help you. Sometimes they simply will not have time to help and still meet their own responsibilities for the day. Also, some family members may not feel comfortable enough with math themselves to think that they can help you. At other times, you may be working on a type of problem that they have never worked on or have not done for a long time.

When someone in your family is able to help, be prepared to work and be cooperative. Make sure that you have your math book at home with you. Your helper may want to read the explanation in the book or look at the sample problems to see what you might be doing wrong or to refresh his or her own memory on how to do the problems. Be aware that your parents may use different terms than you do for the same math concepts. For example, some math students are taught to "borrow" when they subtract; others are taught to "regroup," but they are using the same math concept.

Your helper may also have been taught a different method for solving a problem than the method you are learning. Remember that there is often more than one right way to do a problem. Even though you may have to learn the method being taught in your class, seeing a different way to solve the problem may help you understand the math concept a little better.

Above all, remember to show appreciation for the help you are getting from your family. You are not the only one at home busy with responsibilities.

Tutors.   Math tutors are helpful when your problems are serious or when you need help over a period of time. If you decide you need a tutor, start working with one as soon as possible. If you meet with a tutor a few days before your final exam, you may be too late. You must start as soon as a problem develops.

Also, tutors can cost money. The longer you wait to get help, the more money you may have to spend catching up with your studies.

If you need a tutor, your teacher or school counselor might be able to help you find one. Schools often keep a list of people who are qualified to tutor in various subjects. Generally tutors charge by the hour. You should check on the fee when you call to set up an appointment.

Some schools arrange for older students to tutor younger students. Sometimes student tutors are earning extra credits for helping others. If the tutoring is done outside school, student tutors may charge a small fee, but it will probably be much less than a professional's fee. If the tutoring is done inside the school during breaks or recess, it is often free.

No matter who your tutor is, you should go to the session prepared. That means having your books, assignments, paper, and pencils with you. It also means knowing what your problem is. It won't be much help if you greet the tutor with "I don't get it!" You must be able to tell the tutor exactly what is confusing you. Be prepared to say, "I'm having trouble doing long division problems," or, "I don't understand how to multiply fractions," for example. That is the only way a tutor will be able to help you.

Remember, also, that you can't expect a miracle in one lesson. It will take time to fill in the steps you have missed. Try to learn something new each time. Little by little, you will add to your understanding of math. And as you improve, you will gradually become a more confident math student.

Self-help books.   Besides your own textbook, there are many books that can give you additional practice in math. You might ask your teacher, your tutor, or your librarian to recommend helpful math books. The bibliography at the back of this publication suggests some books that other math students have found useful. Many of these books are available in school and public libraries.

When you choose a self-help book, check with your teacher, if possible, to see if it is appropriate for what you are working on. Be sure to begin by reading the directions explaining how to use the book. These directions are usually given at the beginning, often in the introduction or preface. Your teacher also might be able to suggest how you should use the book to get the most benefit out of it. You may find it useful to read the section "Reading the language of math" before you begin to use any self-help books.

With these many available sources of help, you should be able to find one that works for you. But *you* must make the first move. *You* must recognize that you need help as soon as problems appear. *You* must ask for help. And *you* must be patient and realize that improvement in math will come slowly. But don't ever give up; and don't ever think that you are out there all alone.

Using a calculator

Calculators are handy little machines. They do computations with amazing speed and accuracy. Calculators are small and easy to carry around, and with reasonable care they will last a long time. One hundred years ago, mathematicians would have paid thousands of dollars to have them. Now you can buy a calculator that will do everything you need for under twenty dollars.

If you have a calculator, you will find many uses for it. But a calculator must be used wisely. As a math student, your main goal is to learn and understand math concepts. A calculator can help you compute answers, but computation is only one part of learning math. A calculator can sometimes be a useful tool for math students. But you must know when to use one—and when not to use one.

When *not* to use a calculator

A calculator is only a tool. It is not a substitute for understanding how to solve math problems. You need first to understand math concepts and learn how to solve different types of problems yourself before a calculator can be of any use to you.

Say, for example, that you want to buy carpeting for your bedroom. You want to figure how many square yards of carpeting you need. Before a calculator can be of any use in solving this problem, you have to understand how to find the area of the floor in the bedroom. You have to know that you multiply the length of the room times the width. If you understand this math concept, then you can use a calculator to do the multiplication. And you should also learn how to do the multiplication by hand before doing multiplication on a calculator.

There are many other reasons why you should not use a calculator as a substitute for knowing how to do the problems yourself. One is that you can become too dependent on a calculator. Many young people have become accustomed to having calculators around. They do not always stop to think that there may not be one available every time they have to do some computation. If you consistently use a calculator for simple problems, you might find that you can't work those problems without a calculator when you need to. And there will be many times when you will not be able to use one.

In your math classes and in other subjects requiring computation, you may sometimes be allowed—or even encouraged—to use a calculator. Other times, you will not be able to use one, particularly when you are first learning a concept. Then you need to learn how to work through a problem doing your own computations so that you understand the concepts involved.

Always check with your teacher to find out whether you may or may not use a calculator. Your teacher is the best judge of when using a calculator is appropriate—and when it is not. Often you will not be able to use a calculator when you are taking a test. And what would happen if you *could* use a calculator, but the batteries wore down during the test? Your brain is still your most dependable tool for calculations. Don't forget how to use it!

There is another equally important reason for not using a calculator all the time. As you do your math problems, you should begin to see connections and underlying patterns in the work. Seeing these patterns will help you to understand the concepts in mathematics better. If you allow the calculator to do all your thinking for you, you will miss seeing these important connections and short cuts. In the long run, this will hamper you in your understanding of math. Besides, some problems can be done faster without a calculator.

Here is an example of a problem that looks, at first glance, as though a calculator could do it faster than you could:

$$12 + 18 + 14 + 16 =$$

But if you look at this problem closely, you may see that $12 + 18 = 30$ and $14 + 16 = 30$. Then the problem becomes, very simply, $30 + 30 = 60$.

$$(12 + 18) + (14 + 16) = 30 + 30 = 60$$

When you can see the patterns in this problem, you can actually do it more quickly in your head than you could on the calculator. You might review "Developing good math habits," which offers more specific information about finding short cuts and seeing patterns.

How and when to use a calculator

Now that we've talked about when you should not use a calculator, let's talk about when and how you should. There are both practical and recreational uses for calculators. Certainly they will be used more and more in the coming years. Everyone should take advantage of what these electronic wonders have to offer.

First, learn how to use your calculator. You might start by experimenting with it. Do a simple problem to which you know the answer, like 3 + 4. As you do several easy problems, you will start becoming familiar with how the calculator operates.

One of the first things you should do when you get a new calculator is to read the instructions. On different calculators you may have to use slightly different methods for computing different types of problems. So be sure you at least become familiar with how to perform the basic operations—addition, subtraction, multiplication, and division. The instructions manual may also suggest possibilities for use of the calculator that you might not think of on your own. Hold the calculator and practice with it while you read the instructions manual. The more you know about your calculator, the more use you will get out of it.

Save the instructions manual. Later you might want to check on something you have forgotten how to do. Or you might want to use the calculator for a new purpose in the future. The instructions manual is also a good reference if your calculator should develop mechanical problems.

Use a calculator to find mistakes. After you have finished your homework, you can check the problems with a calculator to find out if you have made any computation errors. If you find any errors, you can go back to the problem, see what kind of mistake you made, and correct it. Using the calculator in this way actually helps you to learn. If you simply used it to find the answers in the first place, however, then you wouldn't be learning how to do the problems.

Use a calculator for lengthy, time-consuming calculations. It might be all right to use the calculator for some long problems. But first you must be sure that you *could* do the calculations by hand if you had to. Using a calculator in this way could cut down on computational errors that might be difficult to find in a long problem. If you are unsure whether you should use your calculator in this way when doing homework or classroom work, ask your teacher.

Use a calculator to do word problems. Often the important skill you are learning from word problems is figuring out how to set up the problems. If you can use a calculator to do the computations, you can spend more time thinking about methods for solving the problems. Again, ask your teacher to find out if you may use a calculator for word problems.

Use a calculator to explore interesting ideas. Sometimes it's fun to just play with a calculator to see what happens. For example, try this problem:

$(12345678 \times 8) + 8 =$

Does the result look interesting? Try these:

$(123456 \times 8) + 6 =$
$(1234 \times 8) + 4 =$

Can you think up some other problems like these?

There are whole books filled with activities you can do on a calculator. They can be a lot of fun, and they can make you feel more comfortable with numbers. There are some calculator activity game books listed in the bibliography at the back of this book.

You can also use the calculator to play games with other people. Try having "calculator races" with your parents, your brother or sister, or a friend. Make up some problems that have short cuts, like the one you saw earlier in this chapter. Here are some others:

$23 + 36 + 7 + 4 =$

$48 \times 5 \times 2 =$

$\frac{2}{3} + \frac{7}{3} =$

25% of 20 =

$18.5 - \frac{1}{2} =$

Then have a race to see if you can do them faster in your head than someone else can do them with a calculator. With a little practice you will learn to see the patterns and be able to do these much faster in your head (especially the problems with fractions—calculators just aren't much good for them).

Enjoy your calculator. Have fun with it. Use it to check your work. Use it to do word problems and complicated problems with large numbers or lengthy computations. But don't become dependent on a calculator. Your own brain is capable of more than you think it is— but only if you keep using it!

Solving word problems

Like many other areas of math, word problems are not the big mystery that they seem. If you know how to attack word problems, how to change them to a form that you can work with, you will find that they are not really so difficult.

There are lots of ways to approach word problems. You may find that different methods work better for different types of problems. Sometimes you can use any of several different ways to work a problem. Feel free to experiment with the ideas in this section.

Interpreting or translating the problem

When you begin doing a word problem, you must first ask yourself some questions about the problem. What is the problem asking you to find out? What information is given? Is any necessary information missing? If you do not understand all the words in a problem, look them up in a dictionary, or ask someone. You won't be able to translate the problem if you don't understand every word.

Read the problem more than once. Since word problems present a lot of information in a small space, you will usually have to read a problem several times before doing any computations. On your second reading, it may help to read the question at the end of the problem first. Then when you go back to reread from the beginning, you will have a better idea of what information you need to answer the question at the end.

Look for key words. Sometimes looking for certain key words can help you figure out what a problem is asking you to do. For instance, when a problem includes words or phrases such as *greater than*, *added to*, *increased by*, *sum*, or *plus*, addition is probably involved. Words like *difference*, *decreased by*, *less than*, *minus*, and *left over* often mean that subtraction may be called for. *Times*, and *product* suggest multiplication. And *divided by* and *quotient* suggest that you might have to do some division. Suppose you have this problem:

> Mary walks 6 blocks to school. On the way home, she decides to take a different route and stop at her friend's house. Mary's friend lives 4 blocks from school, and Mary lives 3 blocks from her friend. What is the difference between the number of blocks that Mary walked going to school and the number she walked going home?

At first glance this might look like an addition problem, and there *is* some adding in it. You have to add 4 and 3 to find out the distance Mary had to walk to get home from school by way of her friend's house. But the question asks for the difference between the walk to school and the walk home. Remember, *difference* is often a key word for subtraction. After you have found out that the trip home is 7 blocks, you can subtract the distance to school (6 blocks) from the distance home (7 blocks). The difference is 1 block.

A note of caution about key words: If you find a key word in a problem, consider it only one clue to solving the problem. Some problems will not include any of the key words we talked about. And sometimes a key word can be used in a different way in a sentence, so that it is not really a clue to the answer. Key words can serve as clues, but there is no substitute for thinking the problem through for yourself.

Label your answers. The answer to our problem about Mary's walks was "one block," not just "one." Labeling your answers will help you to be sure you have found the information asked for in the question.

Imagining the story that is happening

Imagining the story is a great way to figure out word problems. Change the problem into your own words. Try to picture what the people are doing. Sometimes it helps to make up a similar problem in which the people are doing the same things, but the numbers are simpler to compute. You don't have to actually work out this new problem. Just making it up will help you to see what the real problem is asking.

If you like making up stories, you can try to imagine why the people are doing what the problem says they are doing. Put some fun into it and you will take some of the strangeness out of it. Be sure, however, that you use this method only when you have time. It might be very helpful when you are studying at home. You may not always have time to let your imagination wander during a test.

Making a reasonable guess

Sometimes making a reasonable guess can help you get started on a problem. Ask yourself what a sensible answer would be. Then work the problem. Is your answer similar to your guess? If they are far apart, you might still feel that your guess makes more sense than your answer. This is another good way to check your work.

Drawing a picture

There are lots of different ways that you can draw a picture of a problem. It might mean making a map or a sketch of some sort. It might help to make a graph or a table. (See the section on "Using tables and graphs.")

Let's look again at the problem about Mary's two walks. You could draw a simple map to go with that problem:

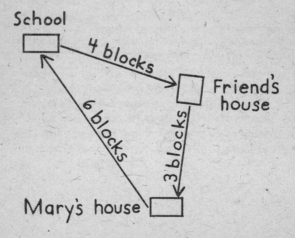

Doesn't this map make the whole problem much easier to see? If you drew the picture first, you probably wouldn't have to do any written computation at all. Just as the picture makes that relatively easy problem clearer, it could help even more for a problem that is complicated.

There are no set rules for how to draw a picture for a word problem. Anything that helps you "see" what is going on is fine. The idea is that when you draw a picture, you can tell better how the numbers in the problem relate to each other. That helps you make up a mathematical sentence, or formula, for doing the problem.

Screening out irrelevant details

In some problems, you are given more information than you need to figure out the answer. These extra pieces of information are called *irrelevant details*. You have to learn to recognize numbers that you don't need and ignore them when you are working out the problem. Look at this problem:

Mr. Weber buys 40 pounds of apples for his store every day. Most days he sells about 38 pounds and takes the rest home. Yesterday, because a terrible storm kept customers home, he sold only 22 pounds of apples. How many pounds of apples was he left with yesterday?

There are many irrelevant details in this problem. Some may confuse you, and some may not. Of course it doesn't matter about the storm yesterday, though that piece of information may make it easier for you to imagine the story. But there is an extra number in this problem that could confuse you if you're not careful.

What does the problem ask? It asks how many pounds were left over yesterday. We know Mr. Weber always starts out with 40 pounds, and that *left* is a key word for subtraction. Which number do we subtract from 40? It has to be 22 because that is the number of pounds that were sold yesterday. And yesterday is the only day we are interested in. The information about how many pounds he usually sells simply doesn't matter in this problem.

Doing problems different ways

There is often more than one right way to solve a problem. If you compare your work with a friend, don't worry if you find that you did not arrive at the answer in the same way that your friend did. As long as you got the correct answer, and understand how you got it, it's fine to use a different method.

Be willing to experiment a little with word problems. Think through each problem carefully. Then use your imagination to try to find a way to solve it. With a little practice, you just might find that word problems are a lot easier than you thought.

Using tables and graphs

Keeping records of numerical facts is one area of math that we use often in our everyday lives. Presenting numerical facts or statistics in tables and graphs can make those numbers easier to understand.

A *table* is a collection of information organized into columns with headings. A *graph* is a picture that makes information more understandable. There are many types of information that might be collected in a table or pictured on a graph. Think of batting averages, test scores, budgeting your allowance, charting your growth. The list is endless.

This section shows examples of a table and four different types of graphs that you have probably seen at one time or another and will certainly see again in the future. Knowing how to read and make tables and graphs will be a big help to you, not only in your study of math, but also in many other subjects and in your life outside school.

Tables

Suppose you and your friends are down at the gym one afternoon shooting basketballs. You decide that you want to know which one of you can get the most baskets in a half-hour. The coach says he will keep track of the baskets for you. In order to do this, he could make a table like the following:

Players	Tally of baskets	Total baskets
Dan	ⅢⅢ ⅢⅢ	10
Amy	ⅢⅢ ⅢⅢ ⅠⅠ	12
Marc	ⅢⅢ ⅢⅢ ⅢⅢ ⅢⅢ Ⅲ	18
Ilene	ⅢⅢ Ⅰ	6

The coach could tally the baskets in the second column as the shooting goes along. One line is made after each name for each basket that person scores. When the playing is finished, the tally lines are counted and a total is put down for each player in the third column.

Tables can of course be much more complicated than the example shown here. They can have many more different lines and columns, for instance. But if you understand the principle of listing the numerical facts in column form, under specific column headings, you can read and use any table you may encounter.

Pictographs

In a pictograph, the information is shown in little pictures. Here is a pictograph that shows the same information that our table showed.

Players	Total baskets
Dan	⊕ ⊕ ⊕ ⊕ ⊕ ⊕ ⊕ ⊕ ⊕ ⊕
Amy	⊕ ⊕ ⊕ ⊕ ⊕ ⊕ ⊕ ⊕ ⊕ ⊕ ⊕ ⊕
Marc	⊕ ⊕ ⊕ ⊕ ⊕ ⊕ ⊕ ⊕ ⊕ ⊕ ⊕ ⊕ ⊕ ⊕ ⊕ ⊕ ⊕ ⊕
Ilene	⊕ ⊕ ⊕ ⊕ ⊕ ⊕

On this pictograph, we can actually count the basketballs to find out how many baskets each person made.

Bar graphs

The information from our table could also be shown in a bar graph. A bar graph can show at a glance how many baskets each person got and who got the most. The bar graph could look like this:

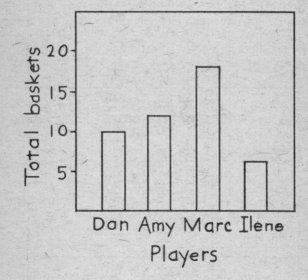

Simply by glancing at this graph, we can see that Marc got the most baskets and Ilene got the least. Everything on the graph is labeled clearly so that you can read it easily. The label "Total baskets" tells us what the numerals going up the left side of the graph represent. And each bar is labeled with a person's name. Clear labeling becomes even more important as you work with more complicated graphs.

Although this bar graph shows the bars rising up from the bottom of the graph the bars could also have been drawn across from left to right.

Line graphs

Line graphs are useful for showing numerical facts that change over a period of time. Temperatures would be a good example. Suppose you want to see how the temperature rises during the morning and then falls later in the afternoon. A line graph like the following would show this change in temperature at a glance.

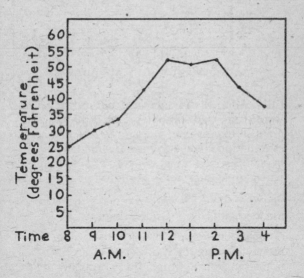

Since this graph is a little more complicated, there are more labels. A dot was put down each hour at the correct temperature. At 11:00 A.M., the graph looked like this:

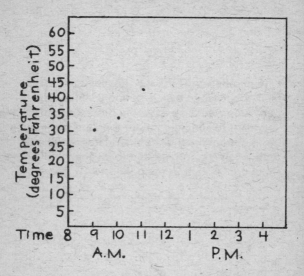

Later, when all the dots were put in place, they were connected with lines so that the movement of temperature is easier to see. (This information could also have been collected in a table. Then the graph could have been drawn all at once at the end of the day.)

Circle graphs

A circle graph is very handy for showing how money is being spent or where money in a budget is coming from. This is probably their most common use, although you will see circle graphs that show other types of information.

You could make a circle graph like the fol-

lowing one to help you see how you spend
your allowance.

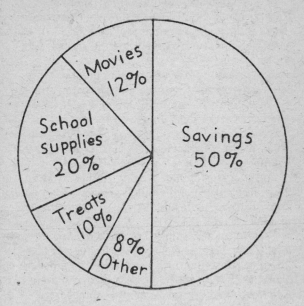

Notice that each section in the circle is labeled
to tell what percentage of the total money was
spent, and what it was spent on. Even if you
didn't understand what percentages are, you
could tell from the picture where most of
the money has gone and roughly how it was
divided. A young child who hasn't learned
about per cent could write the actual amounts
spent in each section.

Notice also that there is a section on the
graph labeled "Other." You will often see this
category in graphs about money. That is because there is always some money that is spent

in different ways each week or each month. In your budget, "Other" might include miscellaneous expenses, such as money spent for birthday presents for friends. In your parents' budget, it might be money set aside for emergencies, such as repairing the refrigerator or the car.

If you want to practice making graphs, there are many types of information you could show. Try to make a bar graph or a pictograph showing your test scores. Chart your height or weight on a line graph. If you want to try something more complicated, get a list of how your county or state taxes are spent. Then draw a graph that shows this. A circle graph would be best, but a bar graph would work, too. Can you think of some other things you can do with graphs?

You might also want to practice reading tables and graphs. Newspapers frequently use them to present information related to a news story. Watch for these in the paper, and then see how much information you can get from them.

Part II

Math basics

How to use Part II

Part II, "Math basics," is designed to help you check your math knowledge. It should help you see how much you already know about math. It may also help you identify areas of math that you need to work on.

"Math basics" is divided into four units, representing four basic areas of math:

basic operations;
fractions, decimals, and per cent;
algebra;
geometry.

Each unit is made up of three parts: (1) a self-test; (2) solutions to items in the self-test; and (3) practice problems.

Start your work on each unit by taking the self-test. Then see how well you did on the self-test by checking the answer key at the back of the book.

If you get any of the problems wrong, turn to the solutions section to find out how to work those problems correctly. Then try working the practice problems at the end of the unit. These may help you decide if you now remember how to do the problems. Answers for the practice problems are also located in the answer key at the back of the book.

If you still do not understand how to work some of the problems after you have read the solutions section, then you probably need to get more help in brushing up your understanding of that area of math. Look back to the unit on "Getting help," and see where you can go for answers to your questions.

Basic operations:

addition
subtraction
multiplication
division

Self-test

1. 2579
    346
    + 83

2. 16
    − 7

3. 482
    −153

4. 534
    −297

5. 7
    ×3

6. 57
    × 6

7. 38
    ×42

8. 547
    ×309

9. 7)31

10. 6)1579

Basic operations:

Solutions to self-test problems

1. *Solution:*

$$\begin{array}{r} 121 \\ 2579 \\ 346 \\ +83 \\ \hline 3008 \end{array}$$

To add whole numbers, first add the numerals in the "ones" column:

9 + 6 + 3 = 18 ones

Put 8 in the "ones" column, and bring 1 "ten" over into the "tens" column. Now add the "tens":

1 (brought over) + 7 + 4 + 8 = 20 tens

Put 0 in the "tens" column, and bring 2 over into the "hundreds" column. Now add the "hundreds":

2 (brought over) + 5 + 3 = 10 hundreds

Put 0 in the "hundreds" column and bring 1 over into the "thousands" column. Now add the "thousands":

1 (brought over) + 2 = 3 thousands

2. *Solution:*

$$\begin{array}{r} 16 \\ -7 \\ \hline 9 \end{array}$$

This is simple subtraction of whole numbers.

                              7
3. *Solution:*   4̶8̶2
                    −153
                     329

Sometimes when subtracting it is necessary to
"regroup." In this problem, you must regroup
the "tens" and "ones" so that there are 7
"tens" and 12 "ones." Then you can subtract 3
from 12. When you regroup in this problem,
you are really thinking of 482 as

$$400 + 80 + 2 \text{ or } 4(100) + 8(10) + 2$$

and then as

$$4(100) + 7(10) + 12$$

to make the subtraction possible.

                              42
4. *Solution:*   5̶3̶4̶
                    −297
                     237

To subtract in this problem, you must regroup
twice. To show the regrouping, cross out the
numeral which you regrouped in each case.

5. *Solution:*   7
                    × 3
                     21

Multiplication of whole numbers can be
thought of as "shorthand" addition. For instance,

$$7 + 7 + 7 = 3(7) = 21$$

6. *Solution:*

$$\begin{array}{r} 57 \\ \times\ 6 \\ \hline 342 \end{array}$$

To find the product:

$$\begin{array}{r} 4 \\ 57 \\ \times\ 6 \\ \hline 2 \end{array}$$
1. Multiply 6 and 7. The result is 42. Write down the 2 below the line under the 6 and "carry" the 4.

$$\begin{array}{r} 57 \\ \times\ 6 \\ \hline 342 \end{array}$$
2. Multiply 6 and 5. The result is 30. Add 4 and record 34 to the left of 2.

The product is 342.

When one of the two factors in a multiplication problem has one digit, the product can usually be found mentally. However, the procedure becomes more involved when both factors have two or more digits, as in the following problem.

7. *Solution:*

$$\begin{array}{r} 38 \\ \times\ 42 \\ \hline 76 \\ 152 \\ \hline 1596 \end{array}$$

76   first partial product
152   second partial product
1596 product

In problems of this kind, each partial product is obtained by multiplying a factor with more than one digit by a single-digit factor. Each time, the right-most digit of the partial product is recorded in the *same* column as the single-digit multiplier.

8. *Solution:*

```
     547
   × 309
    4923    first partial product
   (000)    second partial product
   1641     third partial product
  169023    product
```

9. *Solution:*

```
                4     quotient
   divisor   7)31     dividend
              28
               3      remainder
```

Sometimes when dividing with whole numbers, the quotient is not a whole number. In such cases, there is a remainder.

10. *Solution:*

```
       263
   6)1579
     12
      37
      36
       19
       18
        1     remainder
```

If the divisor has a single digit and the dividend has several digits, we use a procedure called *long division* to find the quotient.

You begin by selecting a *trial divisor*. In this case, the trial divisor is some whole number x such that 6 times x is less than or equal to 15.

There are three numbers you could use: 0, 1, and 2. If you use 0, you have made no progress at all. If you use 1,

$$
\begin{array}{r}
1 \\
6\overline{)1579} \\
\underline{6} \\
9
\end{array}
$$

$6 \times 1 = 6$ product

$15 - 6 = 9$ difference

the difference is greater than the divisor. This will not work. Instead, use 2 as the first digit of the quotient.

$$
\begin{array}{r}
2 \\
6\overline{)1579} \\
\underline{12} \\
3
\end{array}
$$

$6 \times 2 = 12$ product

$15 - 12 = 3$ difference

Next, you "bring down" the third digit (the "tens" digit) of the dividend. You then consider 37 as the new dividend and repeat the "trial divisor—product—difference" procedure. Think: $6 \times 6 = 36$ and 36 is less than 37. Write: 6 as the next digit of the quotient.

$$
\begin{array}{r}
26 \\
6\overline{)1579} \\
\underline{12} \\
37 \\
\underline{36} \\
1
\end{array}
$$

$6 \times 6 = 36$ product

$37 - 36 = 1$ difference

Finally, you bring down the last digit (the "ones" digit) of the dividend, consider 19 as the new dividend, and again repeat the procedure.

Think: 6 × 3 = 18 and 18 is less than 19.
Write: 3 as the next digit of the quotient.

```
      263
   6)1579
      12
      37
      36
      19
      18    6 × 3 = 18   product
       1    19 − 18 = 1   difference
```

Since there are no other digits in the dividend, the final difference is the remainder. The quotient is 263 and the remainder is 1.

As your skill increases, you will be able to find such quotients without showing products or differences. However, if the divisor has more than one digit and the dividend has several digits, it is always advisable to write the steps.

Basic operations:

Practice problems

1. $$\begin{array}{r} 3411 \\ 229 \\ +61 \\ \hline \end{array}$$

2. $$\begin{array}{r} 45208 \\ 321 \\ +16 \\ \hline \end{array}$$

3. $$\begin{array}{r} 2244 \\ 321 \\ 862 \\ +411 \\ \hline \end{array}$$

4. $$\begin{array}{r} 28369 \\ 5432 \\ +10068 \\ \hline \end{array}$$

5. $$\begin{array}{r} 22 \\ -4 \\ \hline \end{array}$$

6. $$\begin{array}{r} 436 \\ -224 \\ \hline \end{array}$$

7. $$\begin{array}{r} 53 \\ -18 \\ \hline \end{array}$$

8. $$\begin{array}{r} 118 \\ -49 \\ \hline \end{array}$$

9. $$\begin{array}{r} 360 \\ -23 \\ \hline \end{array}$$

10. $$\begin{array}{r} 242 \\ -106 \\ \hline \end{array}$$

11. $$\begin{array}{r} 8 \\ \times 4 \\ \hline \end{array}$$

12. $$\begin{array}{r} 19 \\ \times7 \\ \hline \end{array}$$

13. $$\begin{array}{r} 23 \\ \times 74 \\ \hline \end{array}$$

14. $$\begin{array}{r} 810 \\ \times62 \\ \hline \end{array}$$

15. $$\begin{array}{r} 462 \\ \times 831 \\ \hline \end{array}$$

16. $5\overline{)80}$

17. $3\overline{)28}$

18. $4\overline{)261}$

19. $9\overline{)816}$

20. $63\overline{)315}$

Fractions, decimals, and per cent:
Self-test

1. Rewrite (a) $\frac{6}{8}$ and (b) $\frac{18}{30}$ in simplest form.

2. Determine which fraction is greater, $\frac{7}{17}$ or $\frac{11}{34}$.

3. $\frac{4}{9} \cdot \frac{7}{8}$

4. $2\frac{1}{4} \cdot 4\frac{5}{6}$

5. $\frac{5}{27} \div \frac{2}{3}$

6. $7\frac{1}{2} \div 3\frac{1}{3}$

7. $\frac{5}{16} + \frac{3}{16}$

8. $\frac{3}{5} + \frac{4}{7}$

9. $\frac{11}{10} - \frac{3}{10}$

10. $\frac{2}{3} - \frac{3}{8}$

11. $7\frac{1}{2} - 2\frac{3}{5}$

12. Add 28.47, 7.062, and 135.9.

13. Subtract 4.037 from 12.46.

14. Multiply 2.147 and 36.5.

15. Divide 45.36 by 21.

16. Divide 5.6758 by .037.

17. Change $\frac{5}{6}$ to a decimal.

18. Change $4\frac{2}{3}$ to a decimal.

19. Change .125 to a proper fraction.

20. Change .33$\frac{1}{3}$ to a proper fraction.

21. Change 5.75 to a mixed numeral.

22. Solve for x: $\frac{3}{5} = \frac{x}{20}$

23. Change .37 to a per cent.

24. Change $\frac{5}{8}$ to a per cent.

25. Change 36% to a decimal.

26. Change 42% to a fraction.

Fractions, decimals, and per cent:
Solutions to self-test problems

1. Rewrite (a) $\frac{6}{8}$ and (b) $\frac{18}{30}$ in simplest form.

Solutions:

(a) Since $6 = 3 \cdot 2$ and $8 = 4 \cdot 2$, 2 is a common factor of 6 and 8. To simplify $\frac{6}{8}$, you divide both 6 and 8 by 2.

$$\frac{6 \div 2}{8 \div 2} = \frac{3}{4}$$

Notice that 3 and 4 are relatively prime. Therefore, $\frac{6}{8}$ in simplest form is $\frac{3}{4}$.

(b) Since $18 = 9 \cdot 2$ and $30 = 15 \cdot 2$, 2 is a common factor of 18 and 30. To simplify $\frac{18}{30}$, you divide both 18 and 30 by 2.

$$\frac{18 \div 2}{30 \div 2} = \frac{9}{15}$$

Since $9 = 3 \cdot 3$ and $15 = 5 \cdot 3$, 3 is a common factor of 9 and 15. To simplify $\frac{9}{15}$, you divide both 9 and 15 by 3.

$$\frac{9 \div 3}{15 \div 3} = \frac{3}{5}$$

The numbers 3 and 5 are relatively prime. Therefore, $\frac{18}{30}$ in simplest form is $\frac{3}{5}$.
  You could have rewritten $\frac{18}{30}$ in simplest form in one step if you had divided by the *greatest*

common factor. In this case, the greatest common factor is 6.

$$\frac{18 \div 6}{30 \div 6} = \frac{3}{5}$$

2. Determine which fraction is greater, $\frac{7}{17}$ or $\frac{11}{34}$.

Solution: You can make the denominator of $\frac{7}{17}$ equal to the denominator of $\frac{11}{34}$ if you multiply both the numerator and the denominator of $\frac{7}{17}$ by 2.

$$\frac{7}{17} = \frac{7 \cdot 2}{17 \cdot 2} = \frac{14}{34}$$

Now, $\frac{14}{34} > \frac{11}{34}$ because both denominators are 34 and $14 > 11$. Therefore, $\frac{7}{17} > \frac{11}{34}$.

3. $\frac{4}{9} \cdot \frac{7}{8}$

Solution:

$$\frac{4}{9} \cdot \frac{7}{8} = \frac{4 \cdot 7}{9 \cdot 8} = \frac{28}{72}$$

Write $\frac{28}{72}$ in simplest form.

$$\frac{28 \div 4}{72 \div 4} = \frac{7}{18}$$

Sometimes when multiplying, it is possible to simplify before you obtain the product. To show that you are dividing the numerator and denominator by a number, the numerals are usually "crossed out." This procedure, called *cancellation*, is illustrated below.

$$\frac{4}{9} \cdot \frac{7}{8} = \frac{\overset{1}{4} \cdot 7}{9 \cdot \underset{2}{8}} = \frac{7}{18}$$

The numbers 4 and 8 were both divided by 4.

4. $2\frac{1}{4} \cdot 4\frac{5}{6}$

Solution: Replace each mixed numeral with its corresponding improper fraction, and multiply.

$$\frac{9}{4} \cdot \frac{29}{6} = \frac{9 \cdot 29}{4 \cdot \underset{2}{6}} = \frac{87}{8} = 10\frac{7}{8}$$

5. $\frac{5}{27} \div \frac{2}{3}$

Solution: The reciprocal of $\frac{2}{3}$ is $\frac{3}{2}$. Rewrite the problem as a product and multiply.

$$\frac{5}{27} \cdot \frac{3}{2} = \frac{5 \cdot \overset{1}{3}}{\underset{9}{27} \cdot 2} = \frac{5}{18}$$

6. $7\frac{1}{2} \div 3\frac{1}{3}$

Solution: Replace the mixed numerals with improper fractions.

$$\frac{15}{2} \div \frac{10}{3}$$

The reciprocal of $\frac{10}{3}$ is $\frac{3}{10}$. Rewrite the problem as a product and multiply.

$$\frac{15}{2} \cdot \frac{3}{10} = \frac{\overset{3}{\cancel{15}} \cdot 3}{2 \cdot \underset{2}{\cancel{10}}} = \frac{9}{4} = 2\frac{1}{4}$$

7. $\dfrac{5}{16} + \dfrac{3}{16}$

Solution: Since the denominators are the same, simply add the numerators.

$$\frac{5}{16} + \frac{3}{16} = \frac{5+3}{16} = \frac{8}{16} = \frac{1}{2}$$

8. $\dfrac{3}{5} + \dfrac{4}{7}$

Solution: The denominators are different. Since 5 and 7 have no common factors (except 1), you can find a common denominator by multiplying the two denominators. The common denominator is 35. Multiply to make both denominators equal to 35 and add.

$$\frac{3 \cdot 7}{5 \cdot 7} + \frac{4 \cdot 5}{7 \cdot 5} = \frac{21}{35} + \frac{20}{35} = \frac{21+20}{35} = \frac{41}{35} = 1\frac{6}{35}$$

9. $\dfrac{11}{10} - \dfrac{3}{10}$

Solution:

$$\frac{11}{10} - \frac{3}{10} = \frac{11-3}{10} = \frac{8}{10} = \frac{4}{5}$$

10. $\frac{2}{3} - \frac{3}{8}$

Solution: Since 3 and 8 are relatively prime, the least common denominator is their product, 24. Multiply to make both denominators equal to 24 and subtract.

$$\frac{2 \cdot 8}{3 \cdot 8} - \frac{3 \cdot 3}{8 \cdot 3} = \frac{16 - 9}{24} = \frac{7}{24}$$

11. $7\frac{1}{2} - 2\frac{3}{5}$

Solution: Replace the mixed numerals with improper fractions.

$$\frac{15}{2} - \frac{13}{5}$$

Since 2 and 5 are relatively prime, the least common denominator is 10. Multiply to make the denominators equal to 10 and subtract.

$$\frac{15 \cdot 5}{2 \cdot 5} - \frac{13 \cdot 2}{5 \cdot 2} = \frac{75}{10} - \frac{26}{10} = \frac{49}{10} = 4\frac{9}{10}$$

12. Add 28.47, 7.062, and 135.9.

Solution: Rewrite the problem vertically, aligning the decimal points. Then place the decimal point for the sum and add.

```
   28.47
    7.062
+ 135.9
 ─────────
  171.432
```

13. Subtract 4.037 from 12.46.

Solution: The minuend is 12.46 and the subtrahend is 4.037. Rewrite the problem vertically, aligning the decimal points.

$$\begin{array}{r} 12.46 \\ -4.037 \\ \hline \end{array}$$

Since no digit appears in the thousandths place of the minuend, you fill in a zero for this unit, place the decimal point for the difference, and subtract.

$$\begin{array}{r} 5 \\ 12.4\cancel{6}0 \\ -4.037 \\ \hline 8.423 \end{array}$$

14. Multiply 2.147 and 36.5.

Solution: Rewrite the problem vertically, aligning the right-hand digits of the factors. Since 2.147 has more digits than 36.5, write it first. Multiply.

$$\begin{array}{r} 2.147 \\ \times\ 36.5 \\ \hline 10735 \\ 12882 \\ 6441 \\ \hline 783655 \end{array}$$

Note: no decimal points appear in the partial products.

There are *three* digits in the decimal part of the factor 2.147. There is *one* digit in the decimal part of the factor 36.5. Altogether there are *four* digits in the decimal parts of the factors. Thus, you place the decimal point in the product between the 8 and the 3; that is, four digits from the right-hand digit of the product. The product is 78.3655.

15. Divide 45.36 by 21.

Solution: The dividend is 45.36 and the divisor is 21. Rewrite the problem in long-division form, place the decimal point, and divide.

```
      2.16
21)45.36
   42
   33
   21
   126
   126
     0
```

If the divisor has digits to the right of the decimal point, multiply both dividend and divisor by a power of ten (*i.e.*, 10, 100, 1,000, etc.) so that the divisor is a whole number. This is usually done mechanically by drawing arrows or using carats. For instance:

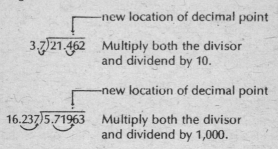

┌──new location of decimal point

3.7)21.462   Multiply both the divisor and dividend by 10.

┌──new location of decimal point

16.237)5.71963   Multiply both the divisor and dividend by 1,000.

16. Divide 5.6758 by .037.

Solution: The dividend is 5.6758 and the divisor is .037. Rewrite the problem as .037)5.6758. The divisor has a decimal part. To eliminate this, you must multiply by 1,000.

$$
\begin{array}{r}
153.4 \\
.037\overline{)5.6758} \\
\underline{3\ 7} \\
1\ 97 \\
\underline{1\ 85} \\
125 \\
\underline{111} \\
148 \\
\underline{148} \\
0
\end{array}
$$

Locate the decimal point for the quotient and divide.

17. Change $\frac{5}{6}$ to a decimal.

Solution: Use long division to find the quotient. The decimal point in the dividend is understood to be after the 5.

Add zeros to the dividend.

$$
\begin{array}{r}
.83 \\
6\overline{)5.000} \\
\underline{4\ 8} \\
20 \\
\underline{18} \\
2
\end{array}
$$

If you continue the division process, each additional digit in the quotient will be 3. You can give the answer in either of the following two forms.

$.8\overline{3}$ or $.83\frac{1}{3}$

The bar over the 3 indicates that it repeats. The decimal is called a *repeating decimal*.

18. Change $4\frac{2}{3}$ to a decimal.

Solution: Rewrite $4\frac{2}{3}$ as an improper fraction.

$$4\frac{2}{3} = \frac{14}{3}$$

Then use long division to divide 14 by 3.

$$
\begin{array}{r}
4.6 \\
3{\overline{\smash{\big)}\,14.0}} \\
\underline{12} \\
2\,0 \\
\underline{1\,8} \\
2
\end{array}
$$

If the division process is continued, 6 will repeat in the quotient. So, the answer is $4.\overline{6}$ or $4.66\frac{2}{3}$.

19. Change .125 to a proper fraction.

Solution: The smallest unit named in .125 is $\frac{1}{1000}$ (thousandths). So you multiply 125 by $\frac{1}{1000}$ and simplify.

$$125\left(\frac{1}{1000}\right) = \frac{125}{1000} = \frac{1}{8}$$

20. Change $.33\frac{1}{3}$ to a proper fraction.

Solution: The smallest unit named in $.33\frac{1}{3}$ is $\frac{1}{100}$ (hundredths). So you multiply $33\frac{1}{3}$ by $\frac{1}{100}$. Then simplify.

$$33\frac{1}{3}\left(\frac{1}{100}\right) = \frac{100}{3}\cdot\frac{1}{100} = \frac{1}{3}$$

21. Change 5.75 to a mixed numeral.

Solution: Express 5.75 as a sum.

$5.75 = 5 + .75$

Change .75 to a proper fraction in simplest form.

$$75\left(\frac{1}{100}\right) = \frac{75}{100} = \frac{3}{4}$$

So $5 + .75$ becomes $5 + \frac{3}{4}$. This sum is $5\frac{3}{4}$.

22. Solve for x : $\frac{3}{5} = \frac{x}{20}$.

Solution: The extremes are 3 and 20. The means are 5 and x. To solve the proportion, multiply the means and extremes, set the products equal, and solve for x.

$$5 \cdot x = 3 \cdot 20$$
$$5x = 60 \qquad \text{Divide both sides by 5.}$$
$$x = 12$$

23. Change .37 to a per cent.

Solution: Change .37 to $\frac{37}{100}$. Rewrite $\frac{37}{100}$ as a per cent. The answer is 37%.

After becoming familiar with this kind of problem, many people omit the fraction step and simply move the decimal point two places to the right and add a % symbol when changing a decimal to a per cent. Hence;

$.17 = 17\%$	$.027 = 2.7\%$
$.01 = 1\%$	$4.67 = 467\%$

24. Change $\frac{5}{8}$ to a per cent.

Solution: Make x the first term of the per cent ratio and write a proportion.

$$\frac{5}{8} = \frac{x}{100}$$

Solve the proportion for x.

$$8 \cdot x = 5 \cdot 100$$
$$8x = 500$$
$$x = 62\frac{1}{2}$$

The per cent is $\frac{62\frac{1}{2}}{100}$ or $62\frac{1}{2}\%$.

25. Change 36% to a decimal.

Solution: Rewrite 36% as $\frac{36}{100}$. Then divide 36 by 100. The answer is .36.

26. Change 42% to a fraction.

Solution: Rewrite 42% as $\frac{42}{100}$. Write $\frac{42}{100}$ in simplest form.

$$\frac{42 \div 2}{100 \div 2} = \frac{21}{50}$$

Fractions, decimals, and per cent: Practice problems

1. Rewrite (a) $\frac{5}{10}$ and (b) $\frac{16}{28}$ in simplest form.

2. Determine which fraction is greater, $\frac{6}{11}$ or $\frac{5}{33}$

3. $\frac{5}{8} \cdot \frac{3}{4}$

4. $1\frac{3}{4} \cdot 3\frac{2}{3}$

5. $\frac{2}{15} \div \frac{1}{3}$

6. $2\frac{1}{3} \div 1\frac{1}{4}$

7. $\frac{6}{12} + \frac{5}{12}$

8. $\frac{2}{3} + \frac{3}{5}$

9. $\frac{6}{7} - \frac{3}{7}$

10. $\frac{5}{6} - \frac{4}{7}$

11. $3\frac{2}{5} - 1\frac{1}{3}$

12. Add 36.50, 3.421, and 126.8.

13. Subtract 12.201 from 20.3.

14. Multiply 6.324 by 20.7.

15. Divide 62.04 by 15.

16. Divide 40.32 by .21.

17. Change $\frac{1}{6}$ to a decimal.

18. Change $6\frac{1}{3}$ to a decimal.

19. Change .625 to a proper fraction.

20. Change $.83\frac{1}{3}$ to a proper fraction.

21. Change 8.25 to a mixed numeral.

22. Solve for x : $\frac{2}{3} = \frac{x}{15}$

23. Change .53 to a per cent.

24. Change $\frac{1}{8}$ to a per cent.

25. Change 81% to a decimal.

26. Change 38% to a fraction.

Algebra:

Self-test

1. Find the sum: $-21 + 13$
2. Find the difference: $47 - 29$
3. Find the difference: $-63 - 14$
4. Find the product: $\frac{2}{3} \cdot 6$
5. Find the product: $(-12)(9)$
6. Find the quotient: $\frac{8}{15} \div \frac{2}{5}$
7. Find the quotient: $-28 \div 7$
8. Solve $x + 5 = 17$ for x.
9. Solve $x - 7 = 12$ for x.
10. Solve $3x = 21$ for x.
11. Solve $\frac{x}{5} = 12$ for x.
12. Solve $3(2x - 7) + 5 = 14$ for x.
13. Solve $8x + 7 - 3x = 42$ for x.
14. Multiply 3^2 and 3^4.
15. Find the quotient: $7^5 \div 7^2$
16. Simplify: $(3^2)^4$
17. Add $3x^2 + 4x - 6$, $x^2 - 2x + 4$, and $2x^2 + 5x - 1$
18. Subtract $2x^2 - 3x + 5$ from $5x^2 + 4x - 7$.
19. Multiply $2x^2 - 3x + 5$ and $7x$.
20. Divide $6x^3 + 4x^2 - 18x$ by $2x$.
21. Factor $5x + 20$.
22. Factor $5x^3 + 35x^2 - 10x$.
23. Factor $x^2 - 16$.
24. Factor $28x^2 - 7$.

Algebra:

Solutions to self-test problems

1. Find the sum: $-21 + 13$

Solution: To find the sum when the signs are not alike, you must subtract the absolute values.

$$|-21| - |13| = 21 - 13 = 8$$

Since -21 has the greater absolute value, you use a negative sign for the sum. The sum is -8.

2. Find the difference: $47 - 29$.

Solution: Rewrite $47 - 29$ as a sum and apply the rules for adding rational numbers.

$$47 - 29 = 47 + (-29)$$

Since the signs are different, subtract the absolute values.

$$|47| - |-29| = 47 - 29 = 18$$

Since $|47| > |-29|$, you use a positive sign for the answer. The difference is 18. (The symbol $>$ represents the phrase "is greater than.")

3. Find the difference: $-63 - 14$

Solution: Rewrite $-63 - 14$ as a sum and apply the rules for adding rational numbers.

$$-63 - 14 = -63 + (-14)$$

The addends have the same signs so you add the absolute values.

$$|-63| + |-14| = 63 + 14 = 77$$

Use the common sign for the answer. The difference is -77.

4. Find the product: $\frac{2}{3} \cdot 6$

Solution: The signs of the factors are alike. Multiply the absolute values of the factors and use a positive sign for the product.

$$\left|\frac{2}{3}\right| \cdot |6| = \frac{2}{3} \cdot 6 = \frac{2}{\overset{}{3}} \cdot \frac{\overset{2}{6}}{\underset{1}{1}} = 4$$

The product is 4.

5. Find the product: $(-12)(9)$

Solution: The signs of the factors are different. Multiply the absolute values of the factors.

$$|-12| \cdot |9| = 12 \cdot 9 = 108$$

Use a negative sign for the product. The product is -108.

6. Find the quotient: $\frac{8}{15} \div \frac{2}{5}$

Solution: The signs are the same. The quotient will be positive. Divide $\left|\frac{8}{15}\right|$ by $\left|\frac{2}{5}\right|$. To divide fractions, multiply by the reciprocal of the divisor.

$$\left|\frac{8}{15}\right| \div \left|\frac{2}{5}\right| = \frac{8}{15} \div \frac{2}{5} = \frac{\overset{4}{\cancel{8}}}{\underset{3}{\cancel{15}}} \cdot \frac{\overset{1}{\cancel{5}}}{2} = \frac{4}{3} = 1\frac{1}{3}$$

7. Find the quotient: $-28 \div 7$

Solution: The signs are different. Divide the absolute value of -28 by the absolute value of 7.

$$|-28| \div |7| = 28 \div 7 = 4$$

Use a negative sign for the quotient.

$$-28 \div 7 = -4$$

8. Solve $x + 5 = 17$ for x.

Solution: Since 5 is added to x to obtain 17, you can subtract 5 from both sides of the equation to solve for x. The procedure can be done horizontally or vertically.

$$
\begin{array}{ccc}
\dot{x} + 5 = 17 & & x + 5 = 17 \\
x + 5 - 5 = 17 - 5 & \text{Subtract 5.} & \underline{ -5 = -5} \\
x = 12 & & x = 12
\end{array}
$$

9. Solve $x - 7 = 12$ for x.

Solution: Since 7 is subtracted from x to obtain 12, you can add 7 to both sides of the equation to solve for x.

$$
\begin{array}{ccc}
x - 7 = 12 & & x - 7 = 12 \\
x - 7 + 7 = 12 + 7 & \text{Add 7.} & \underline{ +7 = +7} \\
x = 19 & & x = 19
\end{array}
$$

It is important to remember that you must always do the same thing to *both* sides of an equation.

10. Solve $3x = 21$ for x.

Solution: Since x is multiplied by 3 to obtain 21, you can divide both sides of the equation by 3 to solve for x.

$$3x = 21$$
$$\frac{3x}{3} = \frac{21}{3} \quad \text{Divide by 3.}$$
$$x = 7$$

11. Solve $\frac{x}{5} = 12$ for x.

Solution: Since x is divided by 5 to obtain 12, you can multiply both sides of the equation by 5 to solve for x.

$$\frac{x}{5} = 12$$
$$5 \cdot \frac{x}{5} = 5 \cdot 12 \quad \text{Multiply by 5.}$$
$$x = 60$$

12. Solve $3(2x - 7) + 5 = 14$ for x.

Solution: This equation contains parentheses. To remove parentheses, it is necessary to apply the distributive property.

$$3(2x - 7) + 5 = 14$$
$$6x - 21 + 5 = 14 \quad \text{Remove parentheses.}$$
$$6x - 16 = 14 \quad \text{Add.}$$
$$\underline{ + 16 = +16} \quad \text{Add 16.}$$
$$6x = 30$$
$$\frac{6x}{6} = \frac{30}{6} \quad \text{Divide by 6.}$$
$$x = 5$$

13. Solve $8x + 7 - 3x = 42$ for x.

Solution: Since $8x$ and $-3x$ are like terms on the same side of the equation, they should be combined first. The sign in front of the term remains with that term. Because of the associative and commutative properties, it is possible to rewrite the equation so that like terms are side by side.

$$8x + 7 - 3x = 42$$
$$8x - 3x + 7 = 42$$
$$(8 - 3)x + 7 = 42$$
$$5x + 7 = 42$$
$$5x + 7 - 7 = 42 - 7 \quad \text{Subtract 7.}$$
$$5x = 35$$
$$\frac{5x}{5} = \frac{35}{5} \quad \text{Divide by 5.}$$
$$x = 7$$

14. Multiply 3^2 and 3^4.

Solution: Rewrite the problem using symbols. Since the bases are the same, you can add the exponents to find the product.

$$3^2 \cdot 3^4 = 3^{2+4} = 3^6$$

15. Find the quotient: $7^5 \div 7^2$

Solution: The bases are the same, so you can subtract exponents to find the quotient. Because the greater exponent is in the numerator (dividend), you must subtract in the numerator.

$$7^5 \div 7^2 = \frac{7^5}{7^2} = 7^{5-2} = 7^3$$

16. Simplify: $(3^2)^4$

Solution: To simplify, find a power.

$$(3^2)^4 = 3^{2 \cdot 4} = 3^8$$

17. Add $3x^2 + 4x - 6$, $x^2 - 2x + 4$, and $2x^2 + 5x - 1$.

Solution: To add vertically, align like terms and add the monomials in each column.

$$\begin{array}{l} 3x^2 + 4x - 6 \\ \underline{x^2 - 2x + 4} \\ \underline{2x^2 + 5x - 1} \\ 6x^2 + 7x - 3 \quad \text{sum} \end{array}$$

18. Subtract $2x^2 - 3x + 5$ from $5x^2 + 4x - 7$.

Solution: To subtract vertically, align the like terms and subtract the monomials in each column. Remember when subtracting to add the opposite of the subtrahend to the minuend.

$$\begin{array}{ll} 5x^2 + 4x - 7 & \text{Think: change the sign of} \\ \underline{2x^2 - 3x + 5} & \text{the subtrahend and add.} \\ 3x^2 + 7x - 12 & \end{array}$$

19. Multiply $2x^2 - 3x + 5$ and $7x$.

Solution: $7x(2x^2 - 3x + 5) = 7x(2x^2) - (7x)(3x) + (7x)(5) = 14x^3 - 21x^2 + 35x$

20. Divide $6x^3 + 4x^2 - 18x$ by $2x$.

Solution: Rewrite the problem as a fraction. Then divide *each* term of the dividend by the divisor.

$$\frac{6x^3 + 4x^2 - 18x}{2x} = \frac{6x^3}{2x} + \frac{4x^2}{2x} - \frac{18x}{2x} =$$

$$\left(\frac{6}{2}\right)\left(\frac{x^3}{x}\right) + \left(\frac{4}{2}\right)\left(\frac{x^2}{x}\right) - \left(\frac{18}{2}\right)\left(\frac{x}{x}\right)$$

$$= 3(x^{3-1}) + 2(x^{2-1}) - 9 \cdot 1$$

$$= 3x^2 + 2x - 9$$

21. Factor $5x + 20$.

Solution: You can express $5x + 20$ as $5 \cdot x + 5 \cdot 4$. By applying the distributive property, $5x + 20 = 5 \cdot x + 5 \cdot 4 = 5(x + 4)$. The common monomial factor is 5. The other factor is a binomial factor, $x + 4$.

22. Factor $5x^3 + 35x^2 - 10x$.

Solution: To find the common monomial factor, you can think of $5x^3 + 35x^2 - 10x$ as $5x \cdot x^2 + 5x \cdot 7x - 5x \cdot 2$. Since $5x$ is a factor of each term, it is a common monomial factor. In factored form, $5x^3 + 35x^2 - 10x = 5x(x^2 + 7x - 2)$. Since $x^2 + 7x - 2$ has no common factor other than 1, you say that $5x$ is the *greatest common factor*. You can check the factors by multiplication.

23. Factor $x^2 - 16$.

Solution: The polynomial is a difference of two squares. The factors are $x + 4$ and $x - 4$.

$$x^2 - 16 = (x + 4)(x - 4)$$

24. Factor $28x^2 - 7$.

Solution: As written, neither the first term nor the second term is a perfect square. However, there is a common monomial factor.

$$28x^2 - 7 = 7(4x^2 - 1)$$

The resulting binomial factor is a difference of two squares and can be factored.

$$28x^2 - 7 = 7(4x^2 - 1) = 7(2x + 1)(2x - 1)$$

Algebra:

Practice problems

1. Find the sum: $-18 + 6$
2. Find the difference: $53 - 15$
3. Find the difference: $-81 - 16$
4. Find the product: $\frac{1}{8} \cdot 16$
5. Find the product: $(-14)(8)$
6. Find the quotient: $\frac{7}{8} \div \frac{1}{4}$
7. Find the quotient: $-56 \div 8$
8. Solve $x + 9 = 16$ for x.
9. Solve $x - 3 = 12$ for x.
10. Solve $6x = 36$ for x.
11. Solve $\frac{x}{3} = 15$ for x.
12. Solve $2(4x - 3) + 2 = 20$ for x.
13. Solve $5x + 9 - 2x = 18$ for x.
14. Multiply: 2^3 and 2^4
15. $8^6 \div 8^2$
16. Simplify: $(4^3)^2$
17. Add $4x^2 + 2x - 5$, $2x^2 - 3x + 2$, and $x^2 + 4x - 2$.
18. Subtract $3x^2 + 2x - 3$ from $6x^2 - 3x + 7$.
19. Multiply $4x^2 - 2x + 6$ and $6x$.
20. Divide $9x^3 - 6x^2 + 18x$ by $3x$.
21. Factor $7x + 35$.
22. Factor $12x^3 + 6x^2 - 36x$.
23. Factor $x^2 - 49$.
24. Factor $32x^2 - 8$.

Geometry:

Self-test

1. Find the perimeter of a square that is 5 inches on each side.
2. Find the perimeter of a rectangle that is 6 meters long and 3 meters wide.
3. Find the area of a rectangle that is 5 feet long and 2 feet wide.
4. Find the circumference of a circle whose diameter is 4 centimeters.
5. Find the area of a circle whose radius is 3 inches.
6. Label the lines: parallel or intersecting.

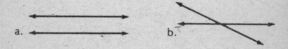

7. Label the angles: right, acute, or obtuse.

8. Label the triangles: scalene, isosceles, or equilateral.

9. Label the polygons: octagon, pentagon, hexagon, or quadrilateral.

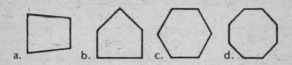

a.   b.   c.   d.

10. Refer to the figure below. Find x.

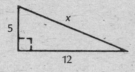

Geometry:

Solutions to self-test problems

The solutions to Problems 1–5 apply formulas for finding perimeter, area, and circumference. In those formulas, the following abbreviations are used:

l = length
w = width
r = radius
d = diameter
s = side
$\pi \approx 3.14$ ($\approx$ means "approximately equal to")

1. Find the perimeter of a square that is 5 inches on each side.

Solution: Apply the formula—

$$
\begin{aligned}
\text{Perimeter of a square} &= 4s \\
&= 4 \times 5 \\
&= 20 \text{ inches}
\end{aligned}
$$

2. Find the perimeter of a rectangle that is 6 meters long and 3 meters wide.

Solution: Apply the formula—

$$
\begin{aligned}
\text{Perimeter of a rectangle} &= 2(l + w) \\
&= 2(6 + 3) \\
&= 2(9) \\
&= 18 \text{ meters}
\end{aligned}
$$

3. Find the area of a rectangle that is 5 feet long and 2 feet wide.

Solution: Apply the formula—

Area of a rectangle = $l \times w$
$$= 5 \times 2$$
$$= 10 \text{ square feet}$$

4. Find the circumference of a circle whose diameter is 4 centimeters.

Solution: Apply the formula—

Circumference of a circle = πd (or $2\pi r$)
$$= \pi \times 4$$
$$\approx 3.14 \times 4$$
$$\approx 12.56 \text{ cm}$$

5. Find the area of a circle whose radius is 3 inches.

Solution: Apply the formula—

Area of a circle = πr^2
$$= \pi \times (3)^2$$
$$= \pi \times 9$$
$$\approx 3.14 \times 9$$
$$\approx 28.26 \text{ square inches}$$

6. Label the lines: parallel or intersecting.

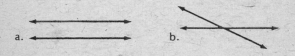

a.   b.

Solution: Two lines in the same plane are either *parallel* or *intersecting*.

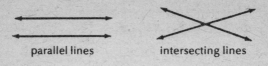

parallel lines   intersecting lines

Therefore,

  a. parallel
  b. intersecting

7. Label the angles: right, acute, or obtuse.

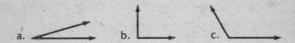

a.   b.   c.

Solution: To every angle there corresponds a unique real number greater than 0 and less than 180. The angle measures most commonly used are degree measures. Angles are classified according to "size."

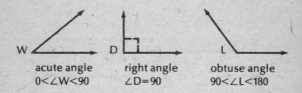

W   D   L

acute angle   right angle   obtuse angle

$0 < \angle W < 90$ $\angle D = 90$ $90 < \angle L < 180$

Therefore,

  a. acute
  b. right
  c. obtuse

8. Label the triangles: scalene, isosceles, or equilateral.

 a.   b.   c.

Solution: Triangles can be classified by side.

scalene:	isosceles:	equilateral:
no congruent sides	two congruent sides	three congruent sides

Therefore,

a. scalene
b. isosceles
c. equilateral

9. Label the polygons: octagon, pentagon, hexagon, or quadrilateral.

a.   b.   c.   d.

Solution: Polygons are named by the number of sides.

| quadrilateral | pentagon | hexagon | octagon |
| 4 sides | 5 sides | 6 sides | 8 sides |

Therefore,

  a. quadrilateral
  b. pentagon
  c. hexagon
  d. octagon

10. Refer to the figure below. Find x.

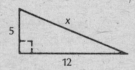

Solution: Apply the Pythagorean theorem.

Pythagorean theorem: If c is the measure of the hypotenuse of a right triangle and a and b are the measures of the legs, then $a^2 + b^2 = c^2$.

$$a^2 + b^2 = c^2$$
$$5^2 + 12^2 = x^2$$
$$25 + 144 = x^2$$
$$169 = x^2$$
$$\pm 13 = x$$
$$13 = x \qquad \text{Measures are always positive.}$$

Geometry:

Practice problems

1. Find the perimeter of a square that is 3 meters on each side.
2. Find the perimeter of a rectangle that is 10 feet long and 2 feet wide.
3. Find the area of a rectangle that is 3 centimeters long and 2 centimeters wide.
4. Find the circumference of a circle whose diameter is 8 inches.
5. Find the area of a circle whose radius is .50 inches.
6. Identify and label the following:

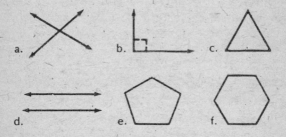

a.   b.   c.

d.   e.   f.

7. Refer to the figure below. Find x.

Answer key

Developing good math habits: short cut problems

1. 20	4. 2	7. 0
2. 9	5. 5	8. 28
3. 120	6. 51.3	

Basic operations: Self-test

1. 3,008	5. 21	9. 4 r3
2. 9	6. 342	10. 263 r1
3. 329	7. 1,596	
4. 237	8. 169,023	

Basic operations: Practice problems

1. 3,701	8. 69	15. 383,922
2. 45,545	9. 337	16. 16
3. 3,838	10. 136	17. 9 r1
4. 43,869	11. 32	18. 65 r1
5. 18	12. 133	19. 90 r6
6. 212	13. 1,702	20. 5
7. 35	14. 50,220	

Fractions, decimals, and per cent: Self-test

1. (a) $\frac{3}{4}$; (b) $\frac{3}{5}$	11. $4\frac{9}{10}$
2. $\frac{7}{17} > \frac{11}{34}$	12. 171.432
3. $\frac{7}{18}$	13. 8.423
4. $10\frac{7}{8}$	14. 78.3655
5. $\frac{5}{18}$	15. 2.16
6. $2\frac{1}{4}$	16. 153.4
7. $\frac{1}{2}$	17. $.8\overline{3}$ or $.83\frac{1}{3}$
8. $1\frac{6}{35}$	18. $4.\overline{6}$ or $4.66\frac{2}{3}$
9. $\frac{4}{5}$	19. $\frac{1}{8}$
10. $\frac{7}{24}$	20. $\frac{1}{3}$

21. $5\frac{3}{4}$

22. $x \doteq 12$

23. 37%

24. $62\frac{1}{2}\%$

25. .36

26. $\frac{21}{50}$

Fractions, decimals, and per cent: Practice problems

1. (a) $\frac{1}{2}$; (b) $\frac{4}{7}$

2. $\frac{6}{11} > \frac{5}{33}$

3. $\frac{15}{32}$

4. $6\frac{5}{12}$

5. $\frac{2}{5}$

6. $1\frac{13}{15}$

7. $\frac{11}{12}$

8. $1\frac{4}{15}$

9. $\frac{3}{7}$

10. $\frac{11}{42}$

11. $2\frac{1}{15}$

12. 166.721

13. 8.099

14. 130.9068

15. 4.136

16. 192

17. $.1\overline{6}$ or $.16\frac{2}{3}$

18. $6.\overline{3}$ or $6.33\frac{1}{3}$

19. $\frac{5}{8}$

20. $\frac{5}{6}$

21. $8\frac{1}{4}$

22. $x = 10$

23. 53%

24. $12\frac{1}{2}\%$

25. .81

26. $\frac{19}{50}$

Algebra: Self-test

1. -8

2. 18

3. -77

4. 4

5. -108

6. $1\frac{1}{3}$

7. -4

8. $x = 12$

9. $x = 19$

10. $x = 7$

11. $x = 60$

12. $x = 5$

13. $x = 7$

14. 3^6

15. 7^3

16. 3^8

17. $6x^2 + 7x - 3$

18. $3x^2 + 7x - 12$

19. $14x^3 - 21x^2 + 35x$

20. $3x^2 + 2x - 9$

21. $5(x + 4)$

22. $5x(x^2 + 7x - 2)$

23. $(x + 4)(x - 4)$

24. $7(2x + 1)(2x - 1)$

Algebra: Practice problems

1. -12
2. 38
3. -97
4. 2
5. -112
6. $3\frac{1}{2}$
7. -7
8. $x = 7$
9. $x = 15$
10. $x = 6$
11. $x = 45$
12. $x = 3$
13. $x = 3$
14. 2^7
15. 8^4
16. 4^6
17. $7x^2 + 3x - 5$
18. $3x^2 - 5x + 10$
19. $24x^3 - 12x^2 + 36x$
20. $3x^2 - 2x + 6$
21. $7(x + 5)$
22. $6x(2x - 3)(x + 2)$
23. $(x - 7)(x + 7)$
24. $8(2x - 1)(2x + 1)$

Geometry: Self-test

1. 20 inches
2. 18 meters
3. 10 square feet
4. 12.56 centimeters
5. 28.26 square inches
6. a. parallel; b. intersecting
7. a. acute; b. right; c. obtuse
8. a. scalene; b. isosceles; c. equilateral
9. a. quadrilateral; b. pentagon; c. hexagon; d. octagon
10. $x = 13$

Geometry: Practice problems

1. 12 meters
2. 24 feet
3. 6 square centimeters
4. 25.12 inches
5. .785 square inches
6. a. intersecting lines; b. right angle;
   c. equilateral triangle; d. parallel lines;
   e. pentagon; f. hexagon
7. $x = 5$

Glossary of math terms

acute angle An angle whose degree measure is greater than 0 and less than 90.

angle The union of two noncollinear rays that have the same end point.

area A number associated with a region of a plane determined by a polygon or a circle.

average or **arithmetic mean** The sum of several numbers divided by the number of addends.

axiom A statement in mathematics that is accepted as true without proof.

binomial A polynomial with two terms.

chord A line segment whose end points are points of a circle.

circle A set of points in a plane that are a given distance from a given point of the plane called the center.

circumference The length of any given circle.

congruent angles Two angles that have the same measure.

congruent segments Two segments that have the same measure.

congruent triangles Two triangles whose corresponding angles and corresponding sides are congruent. Congruent triangles have the same size and shape.

coordinate system A one-to-one correspondence between the set of real numbers and the set of points of a line or plane.

coplanar points Points in the same plane.

degree A unit of angle measure.

degree measure of an angle A real number greater than zero and less than 180 associated with an angle.

denominator The numeral or term below the division bar in a fraction.

diameter of a circle A chord that contains the center of a circle. Also the length of that chord.

element A member of a set.

empty set The set that has no elements.

equal sets Two sets that have exactly the same elements.

equation A statement in mathematics that two expressions are equal.

exponent A numeral that indicates how many times another numeral, called the base, is used as a factor.

factor One of the numbers you multiply to obtain a product.

function A set of ordered pairs no two of which have the same first component.

hexagon A polygon with six sides.

hypotenuse The side of a right triangle that is opposite the right angle.

improper fraction A fraction in which the numerator is greater than the denominator.

120

inequality A statement that two mathematical expressions are not equal.

inverse operation An operation that undoes a given operation.

irrational number Any real number that is not rational.

isosceles triangle A triangle with at least two sides congruent.

least common denominator The least common multiple of the denominators of two or more fractions.

least common multiple Given two or more numbers, the least positive integer that is divisible by these given numbers.

monomial A polynomial with one term.

number line A line to which a coordinate system has been assigned.

numeral A symbol or name for a number.

numerator The numeral or term above the division bar in a fraction.

obtuse angle An angle whose degree measure is greater than 90 and less than 180.

octagon A polygon with eight sides.

parallel lines Two or more lines in the same plane that do not intersect.

parallelogram A quadrilateral that has both pairs of opposite sides parallel.

pentagon A polygon with five sides.

per cent A ratio of some number to 100.

perpendicular lines Any two lines that intersect to form right angles.

pi The ratio of the circumference of a circle to the measure of a diameter of that circle.

polygon A closed plane figure that has straight sides and three or more angles.

postulate A statement that is accepted as true without proof.

prime number A positive integer greater than 1 whose only factors are 1 and the number itself.

quadrilateral A polygon with four sides.

radius of a circle A line segment that joins the center of a circle to any point of the circle. Also the measure of that segment.

ratio An indicated quotient of two numbers.

rational number Any number that can be expressed as the ratio between two integers p/q where q is not zero.

real number Any number on the number line.

rectangle A parallelogram that has four right angles.

right angle An angle whose degree measure is 90.

square A rectangle that has four congruent sides.

square root One of two equal factors of any given number.

theorem A statement in mathematics that must be proved.

transversal A line that intersects two or more lines at distinct points.

triangle A polygon with three sides.

trinomial A polynomial with three terms.

vertex of an angle The common end point of the rays that determine an angle.

Table of math symbols

$+$	plus; positive
$-$	minus; negative
$\times$	times; multiplied by
$\div$	divided by
$=$	equal
$\neq$	not equal
$\approx$	approximately equal to
$>$	is greater than
$<$	is less than
$\geqq$ or $\geq$	is greater than or equal to
$\leqq$ or $\leq$	is less than or equal to
$\angle$	angle
$\perp$	perpendicular
$\cong$	is congruent to
$\therefore$	therefore
$\parallel$	parallel
$\sqrt{}$	positive square root of
π	pi
$\{\ldots\}$	indicates the elements of a set
$\emptyset$ or $\{\ \}$	the empty set; the null set
$|a|$	the absolute value of a
AB	the length of the line segment joining A and B
$\overline{AB}$	the line segment joining A and B
$\overrightarrow{AB}$	the ray from point A through point B
$\overleftrightarrow{AB}$	the line joining points A and B
$\triangle$	triangle

Bibliography

For learning or reviewing math

Quick Arithmetic: A Self-Teaching Guide
by Robert A. Carman and Marilyn J. Carman.
John Wiley and Sons, Inc.

Filled with cartoons and written in a clear,
humorous style, this book is for self-learning or
relearning basic math. Previews and objectives
in each unit allow you to skip what you already
know. Includes practice problems.

The Facts on File Dictionary of Mathematics
edited by Carol Gibson. Facts on File, Inc.

This quick reference for adults includes simple explanations of math terms and concepts.
In an easy-to-use dictionary format, with lots of
diagrams and illustrations.

Arithmetic Made Simple by Abraham P. Sper-
ling, Ph.D., and Samuel D. Levinson, M.S.
Made Simple Books—Doubleday and Co.

A comprehensive guide for self-study and review. Contains sample problems and practice
exercises.

For getting over math fears

Mind Over Math by Dr. Stanley Kogelman and
Dr. Joseph Warren. The Dial Press

Discussion of math anxiety—what it is and
how to get control of it. Brief review of some
math you may have missed in school.

Overcoming Math Anxiety by Sheila Tobias.
W.W. Norton and Compay, Inc.

Looks at reasons behind people's fears of math and ways to get over them. Also provides help in some troublesome areas of math.

Just for fun

Math for Smarty Pants by Marilyn Burns. Little, Brown and Co.

Games and puzzles for children and adults. This book appeals to both those who enjoy and do well in math and those who think they aren't good at math. It's lighthearted and fun, with attractive illustrations.

Games for the Super-Intelligent and *More Games for the Super-Intelligent* by James Fixx. Doubleday and Company, Inc.

These two books contain math puzzles, as well as logic and word games. Appealing to folks who enjoy a good mental workout.

Calculator Games by Michael Donner. Golden Press—Western Publishing Company, Inc.

This book for children explains how to work an ordinary calculator and includes 17 easy calculator games a child can play. Bright, colorful illustrations and an easy-to-understand answer key make the book fun to use.

The Calculator Puzzle Book by Claude Birtwhistle. Bell Publishing Company

This book for children and adults contains 94 different calculator games. Includes notes on operating a calculator and an answer key with full explanations.

Index